The Spoiler

The Spoiler

✦

Revealing the Secrets of Survivor

The ChillOne

iUniverse, Inc.

New York Lincoln Shanghai

The Spoiler
Revealing the Secrets of Survivor

iUniverse, Inc.

For information address:
iUniverse, Inc.
2021 Pine Lake Road, Suite 100
Lincoln, NE 68512
www.iuniverse.com

Cover design by Cathi Stevenson

ISBN: 0-595-29178-3

Printed in the United States of America

To Mom and Dad

Spoiling is not ruining. To ruin a show is to force people to read and review information of what was going to occur in some forum or environment populated by those who clearly do not want to know. Spoiling, on the other hand, is telling people what's going to happen, based on whatever clues you believe you have deciphered, in a place where everyone does want to know the result and welcomes it.

—The ChillOne

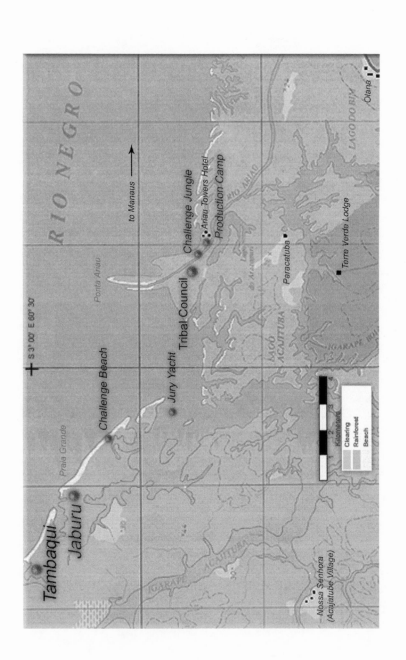

Contents

INTRODUCTION

I've always been a huge fan of the TV show *Survivor*. Right from the original season, I was hooked by seeing a group of regular people, the kind you could bump into at the grocery store, competing head-to-head for $1 million in some awesome location. In fact, one of the contestants in *Survivor: Pulau Tiga* had even attended the same high school I went to on Long Island. That's what drew me in.

Like millions of Americans, I'm totally fascinated by *Survivor*'s social dynamics and game strategies. I still remember clearly in *Survivor: The Australian Outback* how Tina somehow convinced Colby to vote off the more "disliked" Keith in the Final 3, a mistake that clearly cost Colby the Sole Survivor title. Of course, that same season also gave us the memorable scene of Michael taking *Survivor* hunting to a new level when he grabbed that knife, chased down a wild pig, dove on it, and stabbed it like something out of a *Rambo* movie. Once I even auditioned to become a *Survivor* contestant myself, but I never got beyond the initial application phase.

But something happened to me about a month before *Survivor: The Amazon*, something that changed my outlook on this program and my involvement in it as long as the show lasts. During my amazing New Year's vacation in Brazil, I wound up stumbling upon the Amazon filming location of *Survivor 6*, with the scent of the cast and crew still fresh. Only weeks earlier, Survivor Entertainment Group had wrapped up shooting the 39 days of challenges, tribal councils, and the all the other stuff that makes *Survivor* so great. In that same location, I used careful strategy, a fair amount of wit, some intelligence-gathering techniques I had learned from rubbing elbows with professional detectives and "spies," a good bit of luck, and a lot of determination to successfully tap into some of the most closely guarded secrets this side of the CIA.

Then I went public with my "intel." Using the ezboard.com Internet forum SurvivorSucks, the busiest site for passionate fans determined to unravel what will happen in the show before it happens, I revealed several very specific details about the dynamics and contestants of the season. I even named Matt and Jenna as the two finalists and pointed to Jenna as the player who was better liked of the two, providing a tantalizing hint of a possible final outcome! And I did all this over a month before the season premier in February 2003.

I had become a true "spoiler," a role that has turned out to perfectly fit who I am, the work I've done, and the passions that fuel my life. Even as the "flames" hurled at me by my critics sometimes burned intensely all around me, I absolutely loved this unique and unforgettable experience.

For four months, my discoveries and my predictions were dissected, torn apart, argued, debated, applauded, ridiculed, and spun round by some of the best and worst sleuths of the spoiling community. A great deal of the specific information I outlined, especially the identity of those two finalists, eventually came true. But along the trail of the thirteen episodes, some of my information proved wrong. At times I was hailed as a Spoiler God or the luckiest tourist in TV history. At other times, I was mocked as a liar and a villain.

Dozens of my critics in the raucous world of Internet posts even insisted I was just some hoax planted by CBS to toy with the spoiler community, make some news, and rev up interest for the show with carefully timed and controlled information. By the time Jenna was crowned winner and Sole Survivor, however, most of those flamers had their own torches extinguished. After all, in the history of the super-secret *Survivor* series, no one had come forward weeks before a season had even begun airing and authoritatively nailed the two finalists, not to mention countless other details of what TV viewers would see long before they saw them. Still, even today, a whiff of mystery still follows ChillOne.

I am The ChillOne. This is my story.

I won't tell you my real name. That's a secret that I have shared with only a handful of my most trusted friends and allies. But before I walk you through what happened to me on my Amazon adventure, I will share with you a few things about who I am and how I got here.

When I was growing up as a soccer-playing kid on Long Island, I always loved reality TV and the world of spies. I can recall as a ten-year-old how, while watching *Candid Camera* with my parents, I'd laugh at scenes like the cat who sticks his paw into the fish bowl only to get bitten by the fish and scared out of his skin, or the bride who keeps falling down while dancing at her wedding.

Of course, I was an even bigger James Bond fan. I loved all the Bond movies starring Sean Connery, but I fully enjoyed every actor who has ever assumed the role of 007. I was only 12 when I first saw *Goldfinger* on TV with my Dad, but I still remember that line: "Do you expect me to talk?" "No, Mr. Bond, I expect you to die." With all the Bond movies, I loved the suspense and the excitement, the gadgets and technology, the great plots, Bond's Aston Martin DB5, and the cool theme music—not to mention the Bond women! This past holiday season, TNN showed a James Bond marathon. I TiVo'ed all 14 classics over 7 days. After

I got back from Brazil, I spent one cold and snowy day in my apartment in Boston watching 12 hours straight.

I can't say I was actually a spy myself before I sniffed the trail of *Survivor*, but I have done some professional work in support of those who do real spying. While working as an electrical engineer after my graduation from Syracuse University, I assisted law enforcement organizations and other agencies in the intelligence community of several different countries. On one international assignment, I trained police to use a small, portable system designed to record tapped conversations. They even took me out in the field to perform "live" testing, where I sat in an unmarked van while they monitored a drug suspect's car. I won't reveal how that mission concluded, but I can say I learned some valuable lessons during all those days working alongside intelligence professionals.

I also have been fortunate enough to travel all over the world with my varied consulting assignments. In fact, above my computer in my home office I have a 50 x 32 inch colored Hammond map of the world, professionally mounted on a foam board with a laminated finish. On that map I've stuck pushpins at every location where I've visited or lived in through my work or personal travel. I've got 35 pins in the U.S. and 11 in Canada, plus separate pins in Mexico, Bermuda, Ireland, England, Germany, Italy, Belgium, Netherlands, Argentina, Australia, Fiji, and of course Brazil. As a world traveler, and a single guy in his mid-30s, I can say that I already have:

- Scuba-dived in the crystal-clear blue waters off Cozumel, Mexico

- Golfed on the Ring of Kerry, Ireland

- Sampled London's finest microbrews on a classic pub crawl

- Listened to Mozart's Requiem at the Sydney Opera House in Australia

- Attended Easter services at The Vatican

- Sea kayaked off the coast of Vita Levu, Fiji

- Trekked to the summit of Mt. Vesuvius

I figure that all these traveling adventures helped mold me into the kind of "Accidental Tourist" who could fully utilize the opportunity that presented itself to me at the Amazon location of *Survivor*. Without realizing it, I had just been waiting for a chance like this to use my "Joe Traveler" cover to engage in a far more fascinating and adventurous undertaking.

Of course, I probably would never have risked putting myself on the line and boldly probing into the secrets of *Survivor* if I wasn't such a big fan of that program, as well as all kinds of reality TV and spy shows. Yes, I admit I've been hooked at times by *The Amazing Race, Big Brother, Fear Factor, Eco-Challenge,* and sometimes even *American Idol, The Bachelor,* and *Joe Millionaire.* But nothing intrigues me as much as the spy thrillers. I spent hours studying *The Mole,* where a double agent tries to sabotage the players' money-making efforts. And I've often imagined myself in the shoes of the double agent operative on assignment in foreign lands on *Alias,* where the mission is always to retrieve secrets and bring them home safely.

In a way, that was my experience in the Amazon. I retrieved *Survivor* secrets, brought them home safely, and found the right place to share them. Along the way, I tasted all the snooping, the interrogations, the photographic surveillance, the asset identification and questioning, the hiding of my true identity, the action, the adventure, the international location, the language barriers, and even the "playing" with people a bit. At one point I even resorted to…well, we'll get to that later. The only thing I didn't experience was the Hollywood stuff—guns, gadgets, bombs, explosions, car chases, and the like. Maybe some other time.

What's next in my new field of undercover work? I don't really know, and if I did I wouldn't tell you. In my new life, that's now classified information. But I am prepared to open all my files and share with you just how I infiltrated the *Survivor* shroud of secrecy. In a way, I wound up engaged in a reality game within reality TV, and I invite you to re-live now it with The ChillOne. So sit down and get comfortable. Grab your favorite reality TV-watching snack. We are about to zoom the camera in on how and where it all began…

THE SPOILER

1

THE RIO TIP

I got my first tip about *Survivor* in the bar of the Luxor Regente Hotel on the Copacabana in Rio de Janeiro a few days before New Year's.

I had just checked in about midday, a few days after my buddies had arrived for our holiday excursion. I found their note in the room: "At Ipanema! Meet you in the lobby bar at 5:00." So with a few hours to kill, I quickly showered, shaved, and headed out into perfect beach conditions. Ninety degrees. Plenty of sun. Low humidity. Lots of Brazilian girls in thong bikinis. After my first plunge into the ocean waters, I returned to the hotel at about 4 and got a drink. That's when I spotted the two 30-something dudes wearing T-shirts and shorts speaking English. Eager to have some Americans to keep me company, I approached them.

They were from Chicago, they said. Like me, they had come here because they heard Rio had an insane New Year's Eve party. The guy named Dave was bald, whether from hair loss or shaving his head I couldn't tell. Over Caipirinhas—Brazil's national drink made of cachaça (sort of like vodka), limes, sugar, and ice—we swapped tales of our holiday adventures.

"Rio's just my first stop," I explained. "After New Year's, I'm heading over to Foz do Iguaçu to see the falls. Then I'm going into the Amazon for a couple of days."

"No kidding," Dave responded. "We just got back from spending Christmas in the Amazon. We stayed at the Acajatuba Lodge right off the Rio Negro. Man, the jungle was awesome. We're headed back to Chicago from here. So, where you staying in the Amazon?"

"The Ariau Towers. Ever hear of it?"

"The Ariau? Sure. Very cool place. We almost stayed there ourselves. In fact, I'm pretty sure that's where they just finished filming *Survivor*, you know?"

"Really! I watch *Survivor* all the time. I knew the next season was going to be in the Amazon from the promos at the end of *Survivor 5*, but I had no idea where."

Maybe I can shoot some photos of the sites where they did the filming and the contestants stayed in their tribal camps, I thought to myself. And who knows what else I might see or hear? I just might poke around, ask some questions, and see what happens. Could be a real bonus to what was already looking like an awesome New Year's trip.

That's as far as any fantasies about "spying" on *Survivor* went in that moment. These guys from Chicago had sparked something, but I immediately remembered a basic lesson I had learned from observing covert operatives from James Bond to the real field agents I assisted in my consulting work. That is, never completely trust a tip from a source until it can be confirmed or verified. The Amazon is a huge region of Brazil and these guys didn't actually stay at the Ariau Towers themselves. They heard something, but they could be mistaken. It was third-hand information at best. Could be true, but might not be. I wouldn't know until I got there, and there wasn't much I could do about it until then. So I decided to do what any real spy in my situation would do: Keep the tip in mind and be ready to act on it if and when it pans out. In the meantime, fully enjoy the experience you happen to find yourself in. That's one thing 007 always excelled at.

That would be no problem for me. In a few minutes my friends Shep Dog, K-Flex, The O.D.D., and Taff showed up. I had known them from way back when, and all but Taff were nicknamed after hip-hop artists. Soon, our time together was all about clubs, parties, the beach, and chatting up all the ladies. A true man's-man vacation. We were staying in a great hotel on the beach, and two or three million people were rolling in for the big New Year's Eve bash in a couple of nights. As I soon discovered, the food was awesome and the prices dirt-cheap. The weather stayed beach-hot. And the red-light district in Rio was almost as wild and bizarre as the red-light district in Amsterdam.

We had thought up the idea for this New Year's adventure back in June. We were hanging out at our rented beach house in Kismet, Fire Island, something we did together every summer. I was sitting around with K-Flex, The O.D.D., and Shep Dog talking about what to do for New Year's Eve.

"I've always thought New Year's was the most over-rated holiday," I said. "Most years I just go to a bar and watch the ball drop on Times Square and get home by 1. The past several years have been pretty routine and just lame."

"Yeah, I'm sick of going to some jam-packed bar in NYC," Shep Dog echoed. "Let's do something different. Let's go somewhere."

"Dude, I'm all about traveling," K-Flex chimed in. "Let's go international."

"What about Rio?" The O.D.D. suggested.

And that was it. We knew Rio de Janeiro was known for throwing the world's biggest New Year's celebration. It wasn't that far. It was an easy flight. With little debate, it was a done deal. I had always wanted to check out Rio myself and was amazed that I hadn't thought of it long before that moment, but I was pumped that it was going to happen at last.

And I wasn't disappointed. After my friends and I parted company with the two guys from Chicago at the hotel bar, they started showing me around. In the next couple of days we settled on our favorite restaurant, Cervantes, where you could get the best steak sandwich you'll ever taste, with real Brazilian filet mignon smothered with cheese and pineapple, for about three bucks. And we spent long hours at The Balcony Bar, an open-air establishment overlooking the beach that was all of Rio wrapped up in one spot: great outdoor, street-side patio, lively atmosphere, hottie waitresses, ho's looking for work, and *cervejas* (beers) so cheap that when the four of us hung out boozing for three or four hours, the total bill would be less than $20. And, the visual entertainment was priceless.

On New Year's Eve day, the three-mile stretch of beach on the Copacabana was getting cranked for the party. They had stages set up about every half mile, with rock music and Brazilian acts keeping things loud and lively. Lots of Brazilian guys were playing hacky-sack with soccer balls on the beach, and some topless Brazilian women adorned the scenery. I spotted tourists from at least ten different countries. The whole beach area was closed to traffic from 9 a.m. on. The restaurants and bars were steaming with excitement, and the prices were still amazing. We ate more of that Brazilian barbecue they carve right at your table, drank more beers, and watched the crowd roll in.

Part of the tradition in Rio on New Year's Eve is that everyone wears white, so we obliged. Dressed in our shorts and white T-shirts, we took our place on the beach as evening rolled in. The sight of all that white glowing in the dark was just amazing, and at midnight I watched the most incredible fireworks display I had ever seen. They shot them off from a bunch of barges spread out across the three miles of beach. Champagne corks were popping all over the place, with loud talking and singing in a bunch of different languages filling the air well into the night. Man, what a killer choice! New Year's in Rio was everything it had been hyped up to be.

The next day, my buddies and I were getting ready to go off in separate directions. Back when our plans for the trip were coming together, I wound up with a somewhat different itinerary than the rest of the guys because I wanted to use a free ticket from my frequent flyer miles on Continental and they had limited availability over the holiday period. That's why I had flown in a few days later, and I'd be going back a few days after my buddies left. They were leaving for home January 3rd, but I wasn't going back until the 7th. But I wouldn't be staying in Rio.

Around Thanksgiving I had begun thinking about those extra days I would have in Brazil after my friends left. I decided that I really didn't want to stay in Rio the whole time. Where should I go? The Amazon, of course! After taking in so many big cities all over the world, I had been cultivating a stronger interest in eco-travel and the Amazon just seemed to fit. So I went online and found a Miami-based travel agency that specializes in Brazil packages. They recommended that I go to Manaus, the most centrally located city in the Amazon region. Then a coworker who had been to South America said I also should check out a place called Iguassu Falls.

With these goals on the table, my travel agency steered me toward an airline pass that allowed me to fly around to as many as five places in Brazil on one fare. They also gave me three options for a hotel in the Amazon region. The Ariau Towers was an easy choice because the marketing material mentioned that Bill Gates, President Jimmy Carter, Kevin Costner, and princes and princesses from all over the world stayed there. It was the Ritz-Carlton of the Amazon!

So on January 2nd I bid farewell to my friends and departed Rio for Foz do Iguaçu, the town where the falls are located. As major waterfalls go, the Iguassu Falls are a little like Niagara Falls because they also border on two countries. But instead of the U.S. and Canada, I was straddling the border of Brazil and Argentina, with Paraguay pressing in to the west. When I arrived in late afternoon, my tour guide said I should wait until morning to head to the falls. He directed me to a restaurant where I devoured more Brazilian barbecue and enjoyed a hot Latin floor show.

As soon as I arrived at the falls the next morning, I could see they weren't like Niagara at all. Instead of one mammoth drop of a falls, I was looking over a two- or three-mile stretch of a long fall, with lush and unusual vegetation sandwiched all around the cascading water. It was just beautiful. Starting on the Argentina side, I took a raft ride under the falls and got soaking wet. On the following nature walk, I spotted hundreds of butterflies with as many as five colors on their wings. Many would land right on your hand. Over on the Brazil side of the falls, I did another nice nature walk, all the while in awe of this natural phenomenon.

The next day, it was on to Manaus. I had to change planes in Sao Paulo, which was no surprise since every international flight coming into Brazil and most of the flights from inside the country stop there. After a ninety-minute flight to Sao Paulo, I boarded Varig Airlines for the four-hour flight to Manaus.

Not a bad foreign airline: free booze and a choice of three or four hot entrees. Made me wonder what they got in First Class. The P.A. announcements were translated in both Portuguese and English, and a couple of hours after the first meal and a movie, they served a second meal.

I sat next to an older gentleman from Atlanta who was heading to the Amazon just to fish. He recited the names of all the different fish he would go after, besides the piranha of course. Not being overly interested in fishing, I wasn't impressed at all. Now if Shep Dog, K-Flex, or Taff were there, they would be hanging on his every word. My boys are fishing ninjas.

In Sao Paulo I had picked up the latest issue of *Condé Nast Traveler*, which conveniently featured an article on lodges in the Amazon, including the Ariau. I eagerly read through that section, hoping to find some mention of the *Survivor* production. Nothing. I was a bit disappointed, but I knew this did not mean my Rio tip was inaccurate. The omission of *Survivor* news might have had something to do with magazine deadlines falling well ahead of their release date, or some other factor.

Still, my thoughts were now beginning to zero in on *Survivor*. While I still could not be fully confident in my Rio tip, I wondered what would happen if it *was* accurate. Could I really see some of the places where they filmed? Then again, for all I knew maybe they were still there finishing up. I did not have any information about the timing of the shooting and could only remember that the *Survivor* season was scheduled to begin airing sometime in February.

Flying into Manaus, I was startled by such a large city popping up in the middle of beautiful green jungle and rivers upon rivers upon rivers. It was a bit like seeing the glitz of Las Vegas sprouting up from the brown sand and desert of the Southwest. We arrived about 11:30 a.m. local time. Since I had left my larger pieces of luggage back at my hotel in Rio and was carrying only a small bag, I headed straight for the Arrivals area. I spotted the Ariau Towers sign immediately, and the cute young woman holding it could have passed for the Brazilian version of Julie McCoy from *The Love Boat*.

Her name was Patricia. She quickly checked off my name when I approached her.

"How many people are you picking up here?" I asked.

"Fourteen," she replied in clear English.

"Are they all from my flight?"

"No, three different flights, but they have all landed. You are the first to check in with me."

Patricia told me we would leave in about 45 minutes for the 15-minute ride to the eco-resort where our boat was docked. Then the boat would leave the dock at 1:00 p.m. for the two-hour ride on the Rio Negro to the Ariau. That left just enough time to hit the airport *churrascaria*, which is what the Brazilians call their BBQ restaurant, and a quick stroll around the terminal. When I returned, Patricia had all the troops assembled: eight Americans, two Ukranians, an Australian, and two Brazilians. I soon learned that four of the Americans came from the New York City area: Deidre, who was originally from Ireland, with her travel companion Mike, along with Mike's brother and his brother's Brazilian girlfriend. Over initial small talk, I noted that no one mentioned *Survivor*, but I wasn't concerned. That could just mean they weren't fans of the show or they hadn't heard what I had heard in Rio. I was by no means ready to declare my tip dead in the water yet.

As Patricia guided us outside the terminal, we stepped into a 95-degree day with lots of sun. The temperature seemed fitting for a place only three degrees south of the equator, but the sun surprised me. What about that Amazon rain forest? Weren't we entering the rainy season that's supposed to last for months? Then again, after a four-hour flight I was not about to complain about a little sunshine. We boarded the modern, air-conditioned bus and soon arrived at the Tropical Manaus Eco-Resort, a five-star hotel on the shores of the Rio Negro. When Patricia informed us that we had a half-hour before our boat would launch and suggested we might use the facilities or browse the shops, most of our traveling party headed for the hotel. Not me. I went straight down the ramp to our waiting boat.

She was named the Com Te Souza and featured an upper and lower deck. Picking the upper-deck was a no-brainer for me, and when I got up there I found it was mostly covered except for an open aft section. That's where I claimed my spot, pulling a chair up, taking off my shirt, and soaking up the hot Amazonian sun. About 20 minutes later the others began boarding, and at 1:00 p.m. we left right on schedule. The first thing I did when we were officially underway was to crack open an ice-cold Brahma beer. Ahhh, now that's what I call an Amazon moment.

I was amazed to find how wide the Rio Negro was. I could barely see across to the other side. As I took a closer look at the water itself, I noticed that it was a goldish brown—not a dirty brown but actually quite clear. I had learned already that the waters of the Amazon were very acidic and that mosquitoes did not thrive near them, a piece of very good news indeed.

After a few minutes I pulled my chair up to join the larger group. Lorraine was from Australia, and Irina and Igor were from Kiev, Ukraine. Tim, his wife Lynn, their daughter Megan and son-in-law Kevin all hailed from somewhere in Pennsylvania. The four New Yorkers and the Brazilian couple rounded out the "foreign" contingent. About 30 minutes later, Patricia made her way up from the lower deck where she had been keeping under cover to brief us on our itinerary after our arrival at the Ariau Towers. After checking in, we would have two free hours to roam the resort and its surrounding grounds. At 5:00 p.m., we would gather in the reception area to meet our jungle guides. Dinner would be served at 6 and, this being a Saturday, we could take in the nightly entertainment: a traditional Amazonian Indian music and dance show at the hotel theater.

I noted that the show didn't begin until 9:30 so we would have some free time in the evening. *Perhaps I could use that time to begin making inquiries about Survivor,* I thought. If, that is, my Rio tip checked out.

I grabbed the new EMS binoculars I had bought specifically for this part of my trip. They worked great, but there wasn't much to see. We were miles from either shoreline, surrounded by jungle and too far away to see any wildlife. So I put away my binos, grabbed another beer, and chatted a bit with Igor and Irina. Igor, unfortunately, only spoke Russian. Irina, on the other hand, spoke English very fluently. She also happened to be one very hot looking Ukranian—good company indeed in the steaming Brazilian sun.

About an hour and a half into the two-hour boat journey, the weather started to turn. The skies quickly shifted to a menacing gray, and I could spot the rain on the horizon. Patricia had told us that it pretty much rained every day for the next several months of the rainy season, so that midday sun shining down on us when we launched was much welcomed. Suddenly, I spotted the Ariau in the distance. From my information on the resort, I knew that the Ariau Amazon Towers features eight, five-story cylindrical structures where the rooms are located. Grabbing my binoculars, I could make out the tops of those towers, which were painted green to blend with the jungle. Tower 8 was in full view.

Then I felt the first pelts of rain. Back went the binoculars. Within seconds, the rain was coming down in buckets, much of it striking us sideways. So this is what they meant by the rainy season, I thought.

"Don't worry," said Patricia. "These rains only last 15 minutes. They blow in and they blow out. Just hang in there."

The Com Te Souza pulled into the dock as the torrents of rain continued. When we came to a stop, nobody was anxious to get out. So we waited and, sure enough, the rain amazingly halted 15 minutes after it had begun. It was nice to have the locals to clue us in on the ways of the Amazon.

When we docked, I was the first one off the boat. The air was much more humid than in Manaus, but the skies already had begun to clear. I could see that we definitely were in the low water season, with the river beginning its slow rise at the start of the annual Amazon River pulsation period. There was about a 45 foot difference between the low and high-water seasons, which meant we had to walk up a bunch of steps to get up to the wooden walkway.

The climb must have been at least 35 feet. As I walked across the slippery wooden dock, I was struck by the sight of two large, towering structures in front of me. Tower 8 was to the left and the Ariau's theater, the Straw Hat Building, to the right. Approaching the stairs, I noticed a group of people in traditional Indian attire waiting to greet us. When I reached the top, I was met by an Amazonian tribeswoman.

"Welcome to Ariau Towers," she announced as she handed me a hand-made beaded necklace.

Her gesture reminded me of how tourists get draped by a lei upon arrival in Hawaii. As I walked across the elevated, covered catwalk, I kept staring at all those towers. How could they stand when they looked so wobbly on those shaky-looking stilts? Thin and pointing haphazardly at different angles, the supports looked like they could have been thrown up by some kindergarten kid with building blocks.

About 100 yards down the walkway, I turned toward the main facility. Looking around, I got my first taste of jungle fauna. Four colorful parrots flew across the jungle floor. Several friendly-looking monkeys were running along the rails of the catwalks, close enough to touch if you chose to. As I glanced at a nearby tree, I spotted an anaconda. This is what I thought the Amazon would look like, and my hotel was carved right out of the middle of it!

My eyes continued to dart in all directions as I walked closer to the main facility. I approached the wooden sign standing on two tall supports that announced Ariau Amazon Towers. Approaching the open-air lobby, I passed the swimming pool, where two monkeys wandered along each side munching on fruit. Then, as I neared the reception area, I saw it: a large, wooden, hand-carved plaque right in front of the main entrance:

Neste Hotel Foi Filmado Survivor Amazon.

Translated from Portuguese, it meant: "In this hotel, Survivor Amazon was filmed." Under those words I clearly could see the *Survivor: The Amazon* logo.

Engraved on the plaque were the names of 21 people, including creator and Executive Producer Mark Burnett and host Jeff Probst.

Game on! My Rio tip was confirmed. Now, my real work was about to begin, and it was going to be far different than what the Ariau staff had planned for me.

2

GATHERING INTEL I: THE SITES

In my second-floor room, I took a quick shower in the bronze water pumped straight out of the Rio Negro and headed out for my first look around the Ariau's facilities and the jungle environment surrounding it. As I entered the reception area, I spotted Patricia chatting with some colleagues at the front desk. I could see from afar that she had changed out of the Ariau-emblem golf shirt she was wearing on the boat ride in from Manaus. Now she was wearing a T-shirt that very conspicuously displayed the logo for *Survivor: The Amazon*, with the word CREW on the back.

Double confirmation! It was very clear not only that the *Survivor* crew had been around the Ariau but that the memory of what was obviously considered an important event by the hotel staff was still fresh. I was hot on the trail!

A few minutes later, Patricia came over to me and my travel companions who had gathered for our scheduled 5:30 p.m. briefing. I didn't want to say anything to Patricia about her T-shirt or ask her about *Survivor* in front of the others. From the outset, I knew that gathering "intel" would require privacy and careful maneuvering. False moves in the early going could blow any chances I had of unearthing any *Survivor* secrets.

As the briefing began, Patricia introduced us to our jungle guide who would be with the 14 of us for the rest of that Saturday night, all of Sunday, and until my departure Monday morning. His name was Enrique. He told us he was originally from Fortaleza but had come to work at the Ariau about a year ago because of his interest in eco-tourism. Not to mention the good tips from high-profile tourists, I thought to myself.

Enrique outlined our schedule. Dinner would be from 6:00 to 8:00 p.m., but he advised us to eat on the early side because we were going alligator spotting that evening. The show at the Straw Hat would begin at 9:30. Sunday would begin with a jungle hike and a visit to an authentic Amazonian Indian village in the morning. After lunch, he would take us piranha fishing. The evening was free, or we could opt for a second round of alligator spotting.

Despite the relatively full schedule, I made note of the potential free time for my "*Survivor* hunting" expeditions. I suspected that we'd be given plenty of time for meals, so I anticipated some open time Sunday before the piranha fishing. Of course, I'd be happy to forget all about that fishing if I had any opportunities to learn about *Survivor*. And that free Sunday night....I began to imagine the possibilities.

First, I knew I had to establish an initial private contact with Enrique. He was the key "asset" here. More than likely, any contact I would make with any potential sources would have to go through him. Like a *Survivor* contestant building alliances, I needed Enrique on my side.

The dinner buffet included an assortment of Brazilian fruits, beef, chicken, fish, and soups. I found it all quite delicious and more than I expected. We ate as a group at our assigned picnic table, with Enrique joining us. As dinner wound down, I noted that we had about 30 minutes before we would rendezvous at the Rio Ariau dock for our alligator hunt. A few minutes after Enrique excused himself, I slipped away from the restaurant area myself.

He was having a smoke when I spotted him, and he was alone. I casually approached and made some small talk about dinner and the alligators. Then I made my first move. Pointing to the *Survivor: The Amazon* plaque to the right side of the reception entrance door, I said, "So what about this *Survivor*? Do you know anything about the filming of the program? I'm a big fan of the show myself."

"Yes, I know it is a big American TV show, but I don't know much, really," Enrique replied. "I was not even here then. My role is with the tourists, you see, and the hotel was closed to tourists during that time."

"Oh, I see. Were there many other hotel employees around at that time?"

"Oh sure, lots of them. The Housekeeping staff and some others...Our boat drivers took the people in and out of their filming sites."

"Is that right? Any chance you could take me out on a boat to see any of those sites when we have a few minutes in our schedule?"

"I will try to help you, but I will have to check on that. I will get back to you."

"Great. Now about those alligators..."

And that was the end of my interrogation. I had uncovered what I most needed to know. Some Ariau employees had contact with *Survivor* personnel and had access to *Survivor* locations. All it would take was one of them who might be willing to share a few details with me. But, of course, that would have to be done at the proper time, in the proper manner.

Just then I saw Irina and Igor heading down toward the dock, so I heartily motioned for them to wait for me. For now, my mission was to assume my cover as your basic Joe Tourist from Boston. There were about 200 of us staying at the hotel and I would need to blend in at all costs.

Even within our own group, I would continue to approach Enrique individually because a bunch of guests talking about *Survivor* could be something that might be overheard by the Ariau staff. While the Ukrainians or even the Australian might not care about the details of the show, I didn't know what to expect from my Pennsylvania family or my New York contingent. I figured that CBS and SEG (Survivor Entertainment Group) probably had gone to great lengths to put a kibosh on *Survivor* information in their never-ending quest for secrecy, a hard-nosed posture that includes strict signed contracts with contestants and crew.

So like any good *Survivor* contestant in the first few episodes, I would need to fly below the radar screen. With Enrique or any other potential source, I could not afford to do anything that might make me appear overly anxious. Like fish, they could be scared away. Strategy was critical. Can't tip my hand too early. I was just a tourist, a big fan of the show. Just curious, you know.

At 7:30 we gathered at the dock. Each jungle guide had a partner who drove the boats. Our driver's name was Pirolito, which translates into Lollipop. Enrique explained that good alligator spotting was done at night because the gators were nocturnally active and more likely to turn up on the banks then. We navigated down a few side tributaries off the Rio Ariau. "You must keep very quiet," Enrique instructed.

The strategy was simple. Maneuver the boat to face into the banks of the river, shine a spotlight into the banks, and look for red. Red meant you had found a gator's eyes, which look like a red laser-pointer when light hits them. Before long, we spotted some red. Lollipop maneuvered the boat nose-in close to the shore. Enrique and another Brazilian staff member were standing on the bow, and as we approached land they both jumped off into the darkness. Within about a minute, they came back—empty-handed. As I noted their bare feet, I was quite amazed at their methods, not to mention their determination.

We immediately backed off from shore and started again. Another sighting, another turn toward the banks by Lollipop. Enrique and his partner plunged into the water again, and this time Enrique came back with the goods. Holding the alligator in his hand, he gave us a quick education on how to deal with this crea-ture.

"Would any of you like to hold it?" he asked.

Of course I said yes, and so did a few others. As I learned, you hold the gator by the snout with one hand, with your other hand grasping its tail. Fortunately, this fellow was only about a yard long.

"We only jump out of the boat when we know the gator is small enough," Enrique noted, "and when Mama is not around."

As our group's nervous laughter subsided, I watched intently as Enrique dem-onstrated the preferred technique for releasing the gator. He began petting the gator's underbelly, putting it into sort of a trance. Only a minute later, the gator was out like a light. Then he placed it on its back on one of our boat's spare oars and let it hang over the river. About five seconds later, the gator woke up and rolled into the water.

"Very impressive," I said to Enrique.

"It is nothing really, once you learn the technique," he replied.

Yes, just like gathering intel, I thought. After we returned to the dock, I walked beside Enrique on the way to the hotel.

"Were you able to ask about that boat ride for me to see the *Survivor* sites?" I asked casually.

"Oh yes, I made a call but the person I need to speak to was not around. I will let you know tomorrow," he replied.

The floor show at the Ariau was entertaining enough, though not quite as exotic as the alligator spotting. When it was over, I lingered at the bar with Dei-dre and Mike over a Caipirinha and then headed slowly for my room in Tower 6, passing through the outdoor lobby with the parrots, macaws, and monkeys roam-ing freely. I took out my hand-carved wooden key and inserted it into the slot on the wooden door with intricate carvings and entered my room.

Yes, the Ariau Amazon Towers really did go to great lengths to maintain the authenticity of being in the Amazon. That's probably what Jacques Cousteau had hoped about 20 years ago when he urged developer Francisco Ritta Bernardino to build this tree-house like resort. Cousteau believed that those who stayed here would leave feeling more inspired to preserve the Amazon and the other rain for-ests of the world. In recent years, the heads of state from countries from all over the world had sampled a taste of the Ariau. It will be interesting to watch over the coming years how world policy might be impacted by their experience.

As I lay in bed, I thought about the day to come. I felt reasonably confident that Enrique would do his best to gain permission for me to see the *Survivor* sites and began making mental notes on how I might use the opportunity if he got the green light. My time would likely be very limited, so I would have to make choices. For sure, I would want to see the sites where the contestants had their challenges. It also would be cool to check out the area where the Tribal Council had met. And it would be especially fascinating to see where they lived in their tribal camps. Perhaps I could even find the rocks they wrote on or carvings they may have etched into the trees to mark how many days they spent there. Maybe I could even find some remnants to take back home with me. Although the post-production crew probably had taken down most of the construction, this was still a "hot" site. It had only been weeks since the filming. Tomorrow….

As Sunday dawned, I noted the weather was holding up. Over breakfast, I clarified our schedule. We were to leave for the jungle trekking from the dock with Lollipop at 8:00 and were due back by 11:00. The piranha fishing would not begin until 1:00 p.m. That left two hours.

As we got off the boat at 11, I asked Enrique if we might go out looking at those *Survivor* sites during the lunch break. As he picked up his walkie-talkie, I tried to appear as casual as possible as I listened to his short conversation in Portuguese with someone on the other end.

"It is all set," he finally said to me in English.

I don't know who gave him the okay and I did not ask. It may have been the on-duty manager, or perhaps someone higher up the Ariau Towers chain of command. I suspect that part of what needed to be clarified was whether they would be charging me an extra fee. I had specifically inquired first about the Tribal Council and challenge areas, and Enrique explained that because those two locations were only a five-minute ride down the Rio Ariau tributary behind the hotel, there would be no extra fee. He had already spoken to one of the boat drivers who knew the locations because he had been a member of the boat crew during the filming. He was going to take us there. Even before meeting him, I thought of this boat driver as my primary source. I felt grateful that he was willing to take the time to help me but not surprised. The service at this five-star resort had been superb from the start, with a staff always eager to accommodate requests.

A few minutes later I met my boat driver. He was a thin, quiet Brazilian who didn't speak or understand a lick of English. Fortunately, Enrique would be going with us. Our first stop was the challenge area, and as soon as I got there I called it the Challenge Jungle. I began taking photos of some wooden ladders and debris that had been broken down but still lay about.

"So what did the *Survivor* contestants do here?" I asked Enrique to inquire of my source.

"Oh, many different events," was the answer. "They had big set-ups with pulleys and ropes and puzzles. All sorts of stuff like that."

Sounded like *Survivor*, all right. I asked a few more simple questions about the dynamics of the show. Mostly I was feeling out my source for credibility. Did he seem to know what I was asking about? Was he answering me quickly, without hesitation, or did he have to think about it? Even though he was speaking Portuguese I could tell from studying his face, his eyes, and his gestures when he didn't know and when he was quick with his answers. I liked him and, more important, I believed him.

We spent about 15 minutes walking around Challenge Jungle and then went just across the tributary to the Tribal Council site. I took more photos and asked more questions. I was careful not to ask about the people on the show right away. I was building up trust first.

"What do you know about the tribes?" I asked.

"Well, you know, they were split up as men and women."

That was real intel. Such a split had been rumored during past *Survivor* seasons but none had ever begun with a male/female split.

"Oh, so did the men dominate the challenges?" I asked.

"Not exactly. The women actually dominated some of the challenges over the men, especially in the beginning."

Again, this was important intel, but I did not write any of it down. I wanted to keep a non-journalistic posture. I needed them to see me as someone who was just being curious.

"That's interesting," I said. "Oh, by the way, exactly where did they have the set for the Tribal Council?"

"Oh, that was right here," my source said as I walked to the Tribal Council spot, the focal point of any *Survivor* season. Then he started pointing.

"The people would come up walking up the path here. They would come up from the river holding their torches. And they sat here. And off to the left was where they voted. And when someone was voted off, they walked that way."

Mostly I just smiled and took more photos. I trusted there would be more, and I was right. It turned out the producers had a makeshift trailer right off to the side where they worked on the set on a day-to-day basis, constantly doing new construction. They kept a crew there every day, even though filming only happened there every few days. If anything broke from the wind or rain, they would fix it in this trailer.

As my source spoke, I also studied Enrique as he translated the boat driver's answers to my questions. Sometimes when the translation would come back from the boat driver, Enrique would volunteer a follow-up question of his own to the boat driver. That was a good sign because it indicated that even though he hadn't been around for *Survivor,* he was getting interested now. At the same time, Enrique did not act in any way suspicious about what I was up to. If he had, I planned to stop my questioning right away. I could not ask for a better translator and middleman in gathering this intel.

I also felt confident that neither of these guys would run back later and blab to their bosses that this *gringo* was asking too many questions. And I noted that my source's answers continued to flow, and that most were quite detailed. He gave no sign of fabricating anything. So far, even a real undercover agent could not ask for anything more.

As we continued pacing around the checkpoints at the Tribal Council site, Enrique reminded me that he had to get back to the Ariau for lunch because of his responsibilities to the rest of my group.

"Of course. I understand," I said. "Oh, but there is one more thing. I would still like to see the location where the tribes were living. I would give up my piranha fishing if we could go there."

Enrique asked my source how far away that location was, and I learned that it was 45 minutes one way.

"I would like to help you, my friend, but I could not take that time away," Enrique explained.

"Yes, I see. Perhaps the boat driver might have the time?" I suggested. I would miss having Enrique's translation, of course, but I wanted to keep the intel flowing.

"Oh, I can check about that."

So Enrique picked up his walkie-talkie again and, apparently, the same guy who gave him the okay to take me out on this trip said I could do it. But I would have to rent a boat this time.

"That is not a problem," I assured him, and the fee was set at $100.

My source also made clear to Enrique that he would not be able to take me to the actual tribal camp location because it was a half-hour walk into the jungle from the shore and he never escorted the contestants there during the filming. So he simply didn't know the way and there was nothing left to mark a trail. Though this news disappointed me, it did not deter me. I still wanted to see the beach where the contestants supposedly landed before they went to their tribal camps. I also understood that I would see a second area where they held some of the in-game and post-game interviews, and a third area where the contestants did some fishing. I could take lots of photos. Who knew what I might come across? Maybe something totally unexpected. It was worth the $100.

"I will miss you out there," I said to Enrique. "Perhaps we can all have a drink this evening so you could help translate what I see this afternoon."

Enrique smiled and nodded. Now I had my assurance that I would have at least one last round of live intel-gathering with an English translator.

So off I went with my boat driver in our small motor-powered boat down the Rio Negro. After 45 minutes we landed on a surprisingly white sandy beach.

"Okay to swim?" I asked my driver through hand signals. I was a bit afraid of getting bitten by a piranha but I already had been told that they pretty much stay in the tributaries and don't go out there in the wide river. When my source motioned that it was fine to swim, I plunged right in. I imagined telling friends I took a swim where the *Survivor* contestants got off to go to their tribes. Pretty neat.

After I dried off, I took some pictures with my digital camera, realizing that when I met with Enrique that evening I could show him a picture and he could ask my source what it was. But after a few minutes it became clear that there really wasn't much more to see—no real remnants of *Survivor*. I motioned to the boat driver that he could take me back.

So this round of intel-gathering was a bit of a flop, but I knew it was right to try. I also made an important discovery. In contrast to the distance the contestants walked from where the boat drivers dropped them to get to their tribal camps, the boat drivers were smack-dab on top of the action at the Challenge Jungle and Tribal Council sites because they were so close to shore. Those boat drivers, including this very source with me at this time, were in a solid position to have seen a lot of important *Survivor* events during their waiting time. Perhaps they even got to see who got voted off early and who stuck around until the end? That was the gold I was really after.

We got back in time for a short round of piranha fishing, and I caught up with the rest of my group at dinner. Apparently, no one was going to choose to go out and look for alligators again. That meant most of our group would probably be lingering around the bar the rest of the night. *Got to stay careful*, I reminded myself. *When I talk with Enrique and my source again, I will need to find privacy.*

As I played with the Brazilian fish on my plate, I thought about the meeting ahead. This was my last shot. I would be leaving at 9:00 a.m. the next day. I would need to stay focused and aware of time, and even though I would be asking more probing and detailed questions I would need to maintain my cover. Just a curious tourist who happens to like the TV show.

Then I remembered how both Enrique and the boat driver had seemed so open about sharing with me what the boat driver knew, and I smiled. It was going to be a very interesting night indeed.

3

GATHERING INTEL II: THE CONTESTANTS

The Ariau Amazon Towers main bar was the perfect kind of exotic setting for any undercover agent to meet with his sources. A jungle-straw ceiling formed a canopy over the open-air circular deck area. Birds were lazily flying in and out. Monkeys were freely climbing around and jumping off railings. If you took a survey around the many tables you would probably find people from as many as a dozen different countries and cultures sipping their cervejas and Caipirinhas.

And I was totally pumped for this most important round of my undercover work. When I had first arrived at the Ariau and noticed that *Survivor: The Amazon* plaque, I honestly wondered if the best I could expect was to take a few snapshots and maybe post them on some website for *Survivor* fans after I got home. I wanted more, of course, but I fully realized just how secretive CBS was about protecting the show. Anyone I questioned might have already signed strict contracts not to reveal anything about *Survivor: The Amazon*. But when I found myself actually interacting with a boat driver who knew a lot about the filming, coupled with a reliable translator, I had been prepared. Already I had my photos and a whole lot more that could go a long way to "spoil" *Survivor 6* by sharing accurate information about what was going to happen on the program long before it happened. Now I was going after the spoiler of all spoilers.

It was just about 9 p.m. I was waiting patiently for Enrique and my source to arrive while having a casual drink with Deidre and Mike, a New York City firefighter. Others from our group had stopped by the table now and then, but most had gone back to their rooms for the night. *Survivor* had come up in conversation occasionally, but no one seemed too interested in it. They didn't even get particularly excited earlier in our stay when we stumbled upon another *Survivor* plaque, this one in the restaurant. It marked the Ariau stay of the show's Post Production Department, and above the standard *Survivor* logo they had posted their own three main slogans. Instead of *Survivor*'s famous Outwit, Outplay, Outlast, they had carved OutDub, OutLog, OutCut. I was fascinated, but the other folks were not terribly impressed, especially when they noticed that dozens of other celebrities who had stayed at the Ariau also had commemorative plaques in the eatery.

Their lack of *Survivor* enthusiasm was good for me because it meant that they would not get in my way of a private talk with my sources. I had a clear track to pursue my targeted line of questioning on my own. I had a great opportunity to gain even more "intel", that term I had come to know from my dealings with government and law enforcement agencies. As my *Survivor* probing continued, it was a word that was becoming easier and easier for me to say to myself. Yes, in terms of intel gathering, everything was shaping up nicely.

As Enrique and the boat driver entered the bar, I told Mike and Deidre that I was going to talk to these guys for awhile about *Survivor* because I was such a die-hard fan. They said fine, they would wait for me at another table.

"Hey, Enrique," I said, as I also nodded to his companion. "Thanks for coming. Can I get you guys a drink?"

So we all sat down to a Caipirinha. First order of business was to thank my boat driver again, in front of Enrique, for taking me on the ride down the Rio Negro to the drop-off point for the tribal camps that afternoon.

"I had a wonderful swim in the Rio Negro," I told Enrique.

"Ah, then you believe us that the piranhas do not like the deep open waters," he laughed. "You are very trusting, not like many *gringos*."

"Should I not have been so trusting?" I laughed.

"You have a few more questions, then?" Enrique asked.

"Yes," I confirmed, turning toward my source. "Did you know any of the people on the show? Do you remember anybody's name?"

My intent was to try to get contestant information and boot order intel without being obvious about it. I knew there was no way in heck I was going to get the entire order that every person was voted off, so my plan was to get at least some information on the first four boots and the last four boots. I figured that those eight people would be the most easily remembered because their boots came at the beginning and the end of the game. The middle period would be more likely to be confusing.

I got my first answer with little hesitation.

"Oh, there was a deaf girl," my source announced.

"Oh, that's interesting," I said. That was big news. I knew that no contestant had ever participated on the show with that kind of major disability before. My intel had just risen a notch.

"Who else do you remember?" I asked.

"Jenna or Jana. She was 22 or 23," my source said. "And a big African-American girl with a strong build, and another lady about 30."

When he paused, I asked, "What about on the men's side?"

"There was an Asian guy, 26. Another guy, Brian, 22. Another guy, 26, with a strong build. And another guy about 50."

It was clear from these descriptions that my source didn't remember everyone's name. But I also figured he was giving me as much as he knew. I could have reminded him that *Survivor* begins with 16 contestants and nudged him into trying to recall something about each person. But time was limited, and I didn't want to seem pushy. Then again, I knew that what other passionate *Survivor* fans would most want to know was the boot order—who gets voted off when.

"Do you remember who gets voted off first?" I asked.

As he began to translate my question, Enrique appeared a bit confused. So I stopped and explained to him the dynamics of the game. I reminded him about our visit to the Tribal Council area that morning and tried to give him an idea of how and why *Survivor* contestants go in there and vote each other off. As a foreigner who had never seen the program, he seemed to catch on quickly. Once again, I felt grateful at having such a helpful conduit of information. When Enrique resumed translating my question to my source, he appeared much more animated as he added in details of what I had told him about the dynamics of the game.

"Oh, the Asian guy is first to go," my source reported after a little thought.

"Really? And who was second?" I asked. I was smiling, showing a fan's enthusiasm. Inside I was keeping score of the critical intel I was racking up.

"Brian was voted off second," the boat driver responded, without hesitation this time.

"And third and fourth?"

"The big, strong black girl. And then another lady around 30."

We were rolling now. As I continued to study my source, he still exhibited every sign of being honest with me. Of course, what I couldn't know was how much this boat driver actually did see during the *Survivor* filming. Enrique had said during our first conversation about *Survivor* that several boat drivers had been used to ferry the contestants and crew from site to site. I didn't know what kind of shifts my source worked or how many Tribal Councils he observed. For all I know, it might have been only one or two.

Then again, from careful observation of how the Ariau staff interacted, I made another conclusion. Enrique and my source seemed tight with one another, though Enrique clearly stood higher on the staff pecking order. When it came to boat drivers hanging out with their fellow boat drivers, I imagined that they talked as freely and openly about their common work tasks as any coworkers. Meaning that whatever my source didn't see, he quite likely heard about from his buddies.

After all, as the *Survivor* filming got on in days and weeks, I was sure it was all the buzz around the Ariau. It was, in fact, the only thing happening on the premises. And as time went on, the general idea of how the program worked would have become pretty clear. Ultimately, it was just competition, not completely unlike a good Brazilian *futebol* (soccer) tournament. Who was going to win this championship? Who was going home early? I'm sure they got interested, and I'd bet that if one person like my source missed a development he would ask around until he found out. Bottom line, I trusted that my source knew what he was talking about.

So at this point I knew I could ask for the entire boot order and my source would have given me some answer. And it probably would be at least somewhat accurate. Then again, why would he or any of the Brazilians watching remember all 16 in perfect order? I could never count on that. Anyway, I knew the ultimate intel was the Final 4, and beyond that the Final 2. Those were the million-dollar questions. And it was 9:15 now and Enrique had told me that my boat driver would need to leave by about 9:30. It was time to go after the prize.

"What about the Final 4? Who were the last four people in the game?" I asked.

"The deaf girl….the 50-year-old man….the big, strong 26-year-old guy and Jenna or Jana."

Wow! You just got the Final 4 to Survivor 6. Keep your wits here. How thorough is this intel? He only knows one of the four by name. What about the other three?

My thoughts were spinning.

The deaf girl? Can't be more than one on the cast. The name will be clear when the cast is announced. Check.

A 50-year-old guy? Hmmm. Most Survivor contestants are much younger than that. There's probably only one, although potentially two who could fall into that general age range. Let's let that pass for now.

Jenna or Jana? Almost a lock that they would only have one person with that name. Done deal.

A big, strong 26-year-old guy? That's a potential thorn in my side. Could potentially fit two, three, or even four of the guys. Survivor likes to recruit lots of strong young guys to do well in the challenges. Got to get more specific here.

"Can you tell me anything more about this 26-year-old guy?" I asked. "What did he look like?"

"Oh, he's big, strong, muscular," replied my boatman, who was only about 5-5 and maybe 145 pounds himself. To demonstrate, he actually stood up and held his hand high above his head.

"And his hair, sort of tight, and parted hair off to the side," my source added, making a sweeping gesture to indicate the part.

This is great! When I see the cast photos I can nail this guy's identity. I've got my Final 4!

At this point, I could see that even Enrique was hanging on the boat driver's every response. He clearly could see that what was being communicated was very significant, especially to me.

"Let me help you, my friend," Enrique said. With that, he walked to the bar and came back with a small white piece of paper, no bigger than a napkin, and a pen. "Let me write this down for you." And on that small piece of white paper Enrique wrote:

Jana—23

guy—26

Sr. A/M—50

Deaf girl—22

This is amazing! My jungle guide has just transcribed what was told to be the Final 4 of Survivor 6. I didn't even have to write it down myself, which I never would have done in their presence anyway because that would have seemed too journalistic, not fitting my tourist/TV fan cover. Yes, this is all going perfectly. Time to take the next step.

"Now let me explain to you more about how the show works," I said directly to Enrique. "When the game gets down to the final two players, they don't vote each other off anymore. Instead, the Tribal Council, which is made of the last seven people to get voted off, vote *for* who they want to win."

"I see," Enrique replied.

"So who are the Final 2 contestants?" I asked the boat driver.

"Jenna and the 26-year-old guy I just described to you," came the response.

He didn't hesitate. Not a second. He knows. He knows!

"And of these Final 2, was there one who was better liked than the other?"

"Oh, Jenna was better liked."

I think I have just been told the Sole Survivor! Wait, he can't know that. The vote is secret. Only Mark Burnett, Les Moonves (President and Chief Executive Officer of CBS Television)*, and a few other people associated with the show know who wins* *until they reveal the winner at the reunion show. Not even the Final 2 contestants are supposed to know which one wins until then. Even if this Jenna was better liked, it doesn't necessarily mean she got the votes. But what I have here is at least a solid clue, an indicator of who MIGHT win. That in itself is huge.*

"Are you sure you want to know all this about the show?" Enrique asked in a somewhat joking manner, snapping my momentary mini-trance. "Won't it ruin it for you?"

"Oh, I'm not worried about that," I said casually. "I've been a big fan of the show for the first five seasons and for those five seasons I've watched it not knowing the outcome. This time, you know, I really don't mind knowing the outcome. In fact, I'll enjoy having the different perspective."

"Well, that's interesting. I can see that," Enrique said.

Okay, Enrique may think I'm spoiling. But he doesn't really know the show. He's not aware of just how popular it is, and he doesn't know just how hard CBS works to keep their secrets about it. If he lived in The States, his perspective would be different. But as it is, I still don't see any sign from him that he has reservations about what he has been telling me through my source. He just seems curious. I'm still safe. Still, best to shift direction a bit here. Besides, my boat driver/informant will soon be going.

"I just want to ask two last questions. Were there any serious injuries?" I asked my source.

"No, nothing like that."

Okay, that probably means no one got attacked by a school of piranhas or had to be carried off in a helicopter for some reason. In past Survivor seasons that sort of thing had been happening, and when I present my intel back home, this is something people will want to know about.

"And was there was any other memorable thing, one event that stuck out in your mind?" I asked.

My source's eyes grew wider. Through Enrique, he talked about a scene with nudity. Apparently, one of the women wasn't contributing too much to the game and they were trying to get this person to be more interactive. Apparently this person said something like, "Okay I'll get more interactive, more than you could imagine." It was obviously more than just seeing someone showering. There would be a nudity event with some girl, he emphasized again. Nice ta-tas.

Well, that's certainly something to look forward to! Oh, and it makes for good additional intel, too, I reminded myself.

Okay, no more questions. No pushing. I've got my Final 4. I've got my Final 2 with an indication of who may be better liked. I've got my first four boots. I've got loads of other intel. Time to wrap this up.

Before I could say anything, another Brazilian approached our table and said hello to Enrique. He was a big, strong guy, almost like a football linebacker. Enrique told me that this guy also had a role in the *Survivor* filming. When the 16 contestants first got there, he gave them an initial survival training about the Amazon.

"Wow! That's cool. What did he tell them about?" I asked.

As Enrique translated, I learned that the husky Brazilian had briefed the 16 survivors on what to expect in the jungle, about the plants and bugs they would encounter, and what they could eat. Basic tips. He even described in detail how certain bugs live inside a nut and when you crack the nut open it's like a worm. It's probably the purest piece of protein out there. He also told them about rubber trees that you can whack against to make a loud echoing noise, a helpful technique for anyone who got lost. Basically, he just taught them how to live out there and what to be careful of—the alligators and the nocturnal animals and such. These were many of the same tips my travel group had learned on our jungle trek that morning.

"Oh," Enrique said, "he says he also was responsible for collecting all the bugs that these people were going to eat on one of the challenges."

So they had to eat bugs? Must be one of those gross-food eating challenges. Still another piece of intel to report on. It's going to be one extensive and impressive list!

With that, the survival trainer left. Before Enrique and the boat driver could move from our table, I pulled out some cash and handed them each a $20 tip. What they had given me was well worth it, of course. They had gone out of their way to help and had genuinely provided me with an extra service—more than they realized. I also figured the tip would encourage them to close the door on our little talk and not mention it to anyone else.

I was just being careful there. I wasn't really worried about them talking up how "this *gringo*" was going home with all these details about *Survivor*. In watching them, I knew that they had a high comfort level about sharing this information with me. Our conversation just seemed to flow and, as time went on, they had gotten warmer and warmer toward the whole subject. I suspect that the initial permission Enrique had received from his supervisor to show me around the *Survivor* sites had relaxed them about the whole thing. Of course, I certainly wasn't going to seek out that manager to thank him or her. There are some things, in some situations, much better left unsaid.

"I want to thank you very much for all your help," I said to my source as he got up to leave. In response, he nodded his head. Enrique remained seated.

"I know it's about time for you to go, too," I said. "But there was one more thing in regards to something we had spoken about earlier. Over lunch time when we went out to the Tribal Council site and the Challenge Area, our boat driver friend told you about another hotel employee, I believe it was another boatman, who actually had photographs of the Tribal Council site when it was set up. Any chance you could still find him?"

Enrique smiled, got out his walkie-talkie, and spoke into it in Portuguese.

"He is not around," he said finally.

"Then it's time to let you go," I said, and then I pointed to Deidre and Mike. "And I will rejoin my friends. See you tomorrow morning at 5, isn't it?"

"Yes, to see the sun rise over the jungle. You will enjoy it."

So I rejoined Deidre and Mike and had one last Caipirinha. I didn't tell them anything about my meeting with my source. Instead, I steered our conversation toward our work lives back home, the jungle trekking that morning, our impressions of some of the others in our group. Safe topics. I had slipped comfortably back into my role of Joe Tourist from Boston, simply appreciating his last evening in the Amazon. Nothing more.

But as I returned to my room, my thoughts were streaming in another direction. I had just nailed critical details of *Survivor 6*, including the Final 4, the Final 2, and a hint of a possible winner! I had gathered all my critical intel in a single day and night. It really was amazing how things had fallen so neatly into place.

And to think it all started because some superior on the Ariau staff gave Enrique the okay to take me on the trail to *Survivor*. I wondered again who that might have been and how it may have happened. The truth is that when Enrique first reached for his walkie-talkie to talk to someone to seek permission, I was actually saying to myself, "Oh shit, this is *so* going to get shot down. I'll have to go about this much more covertly. Nobody's going to get permission to just take me around." But the green light came, and with it an opening to my unraveling of all the secrets that *Survivor* vows to protect at all costs. Was it just a bad call on the part of that manager? Or did Enrique's request not go high enough up the chain of command, never reaching a voice of authority that had been warned clearly by the *Survivor* chiefs not to talk?

Or was it CBS not being careful enough? After all, in all the previous *Survivor* series the whole crew had been sequestered in their own assembled camps, away from the public eye. This was the first time they had based their operation at a hotel. Maybe they thought they had done enough by closing the Ariau off to tourists during the filming and production. Maybe they thought they were protected. Well, when I make my intel public they will be in for a little bit of a surprise.

The next morning, I managed to get up for our group's 5:00 a.m. gathering and sunrise boat ride. We left at 5:30, but we didn't go far down the Rio Negro because we needed to be back at the Ariau in time for breakfast before our departure at 9. We didn't even see the sun rise because the morning remained overcast. As we sat in the boat, a loud, strange noise pierced the silence. *GRRRRRH.* It was something like the growl your stomach makes when you're extremely hungry, only amplified about fifty times.

"What the heck is that, Enrique?" I asked.

"Oh, that is just the gorillas. They are just waking up, and when they wake up they start singing," he explained.

At first I thought he might have been kidding, but as I watched his expression, something I had come to know quite well by now, I realized that Enrique was being perfectly serious. And telling the truth. *GRRRRRH.* It was only the gorillas. For a moment I smiled to myself and imagined their noise actually saying, *SPOILER! SPOILER!,* like something out of a movie.

But, of course, not even the gorillas knew what secrets I had pried from their jungle. Like a character on the TV show *Alias,* I was about to head home safely with my intel. My next assignment: to brief the public with what I knew about *Survivor: The Amazon.*

4

CHILLONE SETS THE STAGE

I flew into Newark and sped up I-95 to Boston at about 80 miles per hour, eager to get home and find the right Internet forum to lay out my intel on *Survivor: The Amazon*.

"I've got a whole lot here," I said to myself. "I've got location information. I've got photographs of *Survivor* plaques hanging in the Ariau Amazon Towers. I've got photographs of the Tribal Council and Challenge venues. I've got lots of game dynamic information. I've got the Final 4 and the Final 2, and I've got a clear signal about the possible winner, the identity of the Sole Survivor. But I've got to post my information fast. Who knows what someone else might have already uncovered?"

When I got back to my apartment in Boston, I threw my clothes in my laundry bag and shoved it in the corner, unpacked a few basic necessities for the next day or two, and charged to my computer. Using a Google.com search, I was directed to SurvivorNews.net and discovered a link for six or seven spoiler sites. I had visited a few now and then during the first five *Survivor* seasons, but I had never posted anything and didn't remember all the site names. I wasn't the type just to go on there to debate or speculate about what was going to happen on the program based on "vidcaps," the name the boards used to refer to shots of CBS promos and selected portions of the show that they would analyze for clues of what would happen in forthcoming episodes. I only wanted to go on if and when I had solid information to share. Now I had it.

As I browsed the sites, I was looking for the most signs of activity about *Survivor 6*, still a month before start date. It didn't take long to determine that the ezboard.com forum SurvivorSucks was the hottest spot. It had a huge spoiling section, where hundreds of people were already posting information about the upcoming season. One spoiler named Wezzie was already putting up photos and descriptions of the *Survivor* site locations. When I checked the statistics on ezboard, I found that they averaged more than 65,000 visits a day, with more than 20,000 registered users.

"Wow, this is it!" I said to myself. "This is my home. Time to get the info out there."

I didn't have any notes from my intel gathering sessions with Enrique and the boat driver. I didn't need them. I had a clear, vivid picture of everything that was told to me. So I just sat down and launched my first post, dated January 9th at 7:13 p.m. Central time, 8:13 p.m. at my home in Boston:

"Greetings,

I have just returned from Brazil and a trip to the Amazon. First off, I have read many threads on this S6, and decided to start my own thread as an attempt to keep the focus and questions here.

I will begin by saying that I do not have all the answers or all the information about S6, but I have enough credible, spoiler type information that I'd be open to sharing.

First off, the map posted by Wezzie is very accurate. Let me start by filling in some of the gaps....

The location of the Ariau Amazon Towers is correct; and yes, the Survivor Production Crew did live there for 3 months. I know this because I stayed there myself just last week.

Now, Wezzie has a big Tribal Council question mark on the map...well, let me answer this question. The tribal council is VERY close to the Ariau Amazon Towers. In fact, it's only about 1.5 km North of the Ariau Hotel; on the West side of the Rio Ariau tributary.

OK, moving on....Wezzie has a table on the map called Challenge Beach. Hmmmm...I cannot confirm whether or not "challenges" actually took place at this place, but they might have. My sources (with whom I will not reveal), did not give me a good indication that challenges actually too place here. What I can confirm (with about 95% confidence) is that the place labeled "Challenge Beach" is where it all began...Day 1: it's the place where all 16 Survivors "landed" in the first minute of being on dry land.

Hmmmm...OK, back to challenges. What I can confirm is the location of one (or maybe the only) challenge venue. This is also located VERY close to the Ariau Towers as well. This location is about 1 km North on the Rio Ariau tributary, on the East side.

OK, now what about the camps. Unfortunately, I was not able to obtain good intel about these locations, but I know that one of the camps is near "Challenge Beach" as documented by Wezzie. My guess is that it is located on the major peninsula where the N-S-E-W graphic is. As far as the second camp is concerned…I'm really not sure. I was told that it might be as far away as the other side of the Rio Negro (which is almost 10 miles wide at this point on the rover). These locations were highly secret as you can imagine.

Hmmmm…well, I think that's enough information for now. I will be happy to answer your questions.

Also, I am not on ezboard all that often, so, please be patient with me. I will check back again over the weekend.

PHOTO 1 (refer to the pages following Chapter 6)

"Thank you" plaque dedicated to the Ariau by the Survivor crew:

PHOTO 2 (refer to the pages following Chapter 6)

"Challenge Beach as diagramed by Wezzie (I was there):

Happy New Year to all.

—The ChillOne"

I registered the posting alias of ChillOne because it was the closest I could come to ChillWill, the nickname my buddy Hep from NYC had given me and all my friends used for me. But that name, another reference to a rapper, was already taken. So were other close nicknames Bushwick, Chill, and B-Real. So I went with the Cypress Hill inspired ChillOne *(known to get ill one)* because it seemed easy to remember, and maybe it had a certain air to it.

In launching my own separate thread on SurvivorSucks, I did not reveal most of my primary intel for a number of strategic reasons. First, since Wezzie already had established info about the sites and others had responded to that, I thought I would enter gracefully by picking up on a trail that already had been set. More important, I had hoped to gain a sense of power by holding back my big intel for awhile. I wanted the spoilers out there to be eager to see what I was going to post next. Yes, like any good agent I was "playing" with them a little bit.

Also, I wanted to build up more and more interest in my thread. I was concerned that by sharing everything all at once, people would just have an initial response to what I said and then wait to see how accurate it all turned out to be. I didn't just want these people to say, "Thanks, Chill" and then go away. I had never participated in a thread like this before and I could see that by playing the role of informal moderator and giving them meaty information, I had the potential to gain a legendary status within the spoiler community. If so, I wanted to keep that up for the whole season, not just for the attention but to add potency to the intel. In undercover operations, that's part of the game.

So initially, I thought I might take several days, or even a week or more to give them my intel about the contestants, especially the identity of those in my Final

4. But it soon became clear that I would have to adjust my strategy. The very first question directed at me asked, "Were you able to get any leads on who might have been on the show?" So I dropped my first nugget at 7:55 p.m. that first day:

"As far as contestants... Yes, I do have information on this as well. What I can share is that you will find your first physically handicapped contestant on S6...a woman who is hearing impaired (deaf). I will share more contestant information over the coming months. I will tell you that I do NOT know the entire "cast list." I do NOT know last names either. I only know the first names of about a handful of contestants and the basic descriptions of a few more."

The tease was on. And with that came the first speculation that I must be some kind of a plant. At 7:59 p.m., Snewser posted:

"What's your connection to the show?"

And at 8:08 p.m., I responded:

"Snewser, I can assure you that I am not affiliated with the show at all...I really just got lucky. My friends and I planned a huge New Year's trip to Rio de Janeiro a while ago (which, by the way, was out of control). Anyway, I decided that if I was going to Brazil and spending 10 days in Rio, why not branch out and see some of the country? I visited Iguacu Falls on the Argentina border and, being the eco-traveler that I am, wanted to see the Amazon..."

With that post, I hoped to firm up my "Joe Tourist" identity to the board. But I didn't go into any detail about how I found my sources and gathered my intel. Again, I wanted to whet their appetite so that they'd keep asking me for more info. It helped that I gained an immediate vote of confidence from Wezzie, one of the most respected veteran spoilers. She verified my site info and concluded:

"If ChillOne has this info right, then I'm going to trust his word about the contestants and other locations. Welcome home and thanks for spoiling!"

Two hours later, still on that first evening, I got another "Good work!" validation from Dan Bollinger, another respected long-timer and location expert who set up maps of *Survivor* locations. But Antithesys, the thread administrator at the time, urged me to reveal my contestant information right away, and even Wezzie advised, "Never sit on a spoiler or it will bite you in the butt."

So, first thing on the morning after my initial post, I told them all that I would "divulge cast information" that night. And I dropped another little tease, letting them know that "the deaf girl" makes it to the Final 4. The reason that I needed to wait until that evening to outline more of my cast intel was that I already had gone back to work at my job as a SAP software analyst for a large defense contractor just outside of Boston. Of course, I didn't tell anyone at work about my covert Amazon operation. I didn't even tell my friends because they weren't *Survivor* fans and I knew they wouldn't be overly interested.

Anyway, at work I couldn't spend the time I wanted to review my memories and carefully craft my post. But during every possible break, and throughout my lunch hour, I kept an eye on the posts amassing on my SurvivorSucks thread. Of course, in those first few days on SurvivorSucks there also might have been a few other "stolen moments" of thread-watching that I'd rather not have my employer know about. By lunch time that day, several more non-believers had lined up to accuse me of being a plant, or even MB himself. I quickly learned that MB were the initials that *Survivor* creator Mark Burnett was usually referred to by some spoilers. So in a quick post I announced:

"Believe what you wish, but, I am not (nor do I know) who MB is. This is a spoiler site and I am sure you have many doubts about what you read and/or see. That is fine by me.

I am confident that my sources in the Amazon were sincere and provided me with the best information possible and to the best of their memory…"

As calm as I sounded publicly toward this initial questioning, privately I was surprised. Oh, I knew I'd get some of those other kinds of spoilers, those who want to "spoil the spoiler." There would certainly be non-believers. But I didn't expect the large number of "flamers" that came out and immediately pegged me as a plant that was sabotaging the group with deception. I kept wondering why they were even here. After all, wasn't this a spoiling board? I figured most people would love my information. Then it struck me—maybe *they* were working for Mark Burnett and CBS by trying to undermine my credibility so that no one would believe me and wouldn't know what really happens on the show. In the world of intelligence operations, there are spies and then there are counterspies. You always have to watch your back. Even if these conspiracy theorists weren't really double agents, this anti-spoiling would be something I would just have to deal with.

At home that night, I decided to go back to my initial vehicle for building credibility. I posted five more photos, including shots of the Tribal Council site and Challenge Jungle. Then, as I began my next post on cast intel, I thought carefully about the right approach. If I went right to my Final 4, the board would not pay much attention to my other intel. So I would build up to that in install-ments, while handing them plenty to chew on. So at 6:09 p.m., on January 10th, I posted:

"Here is what I know…it's not much.
Women:

Deaf contestant, 22.

Jana or Jenna, 23

Joanna (African American); strong build

Another lady around 30

Men:

Daniel, 26 (Asian)

Brian, 22

Another guy, 26; "strong build"

Another guy, 50

OK, OK, I know it's not much, but, as I mentioned, I was trying to see more of the sites and had some communication barriers.

I guess I get some low marks on this information, huh...

Anyway, additional information:

The 16 WILL start off as 2 tribes...split by men and women. They will live and compete initially as men and women. It is my understanding that the groups will merge much earlier...possibly after the first 3 or 4 contestants are gone.

From a challenge perspective, the women dominate in the beginning and it causes great tension amongst the male tribe members. The first 2 voted off are men.

Anyway, ENJOY!!! I am off to NYC to see my brother's band play. I will be back on tomorrow afternoon to address all questions and comments as I know there will be many. Bear with me...

—The ChillOne"

I chose to emphasize the male/female split because in S1-S5 (that's the abbreviation of *Survivor* seasons routinely used by the board), the tribes had always been coed. I had noticed some previous speculation among the spoilers that a gender tribe split in S6 would be an interesting twist to the game, but it was just idle chit-chat then. So for me to come along now and confirm that this would actually happen was a way to build on my credentials, just as pointing to *Survivor*'s first deaf contestant had done. I spoiled these things first to hit a "home run" right from the start.

Also, I downplayed the importance of what I knew ("it's not much") and continued to hold back the order of the first four boots and the Final 4 so as to continue to play mind games with them and add to the intrigue. I wanted my main intel to have a major build-up. And with that, as the post indicates, I really did dash off to New York City to see my brother's gig. And he totally jammed!

While I was gone, the reaction to my news about the male/female tribe split kept the posts flowing practically through the night. I also found several direct questions posed to me regarding the nature of the gender split and some of the details about my new photos. I responded to those questions early afternoon on the 11th, a Saturday.

Taking this posture of answering questions directly was a major part of my strategy. From studying the spoiler community, I knew that most past spoilers would come on and post their info and then sort of disappear, especially when any of their information proved to be inaccurate. From the outset, I decided that I would be different. If they asked me something I knew, I would provide the information. If they asked me something I didn't know, I would tell them I didn't know. And if and when any of my intel didn't pan out, I would hold firm, admit to the inaccuracy, take the heat, and stick around. In this way, I would prove my integrity. Those who visited my thread would know I was a spoiler worthy of the name.

Later that afternoon, one poster asked if I was a cameraman for *Survivor*. "Are you my Uncle?" asked iceball002. This was a reference to the famous Uncle Camerman (yes, it was spelled that way), the posting name of a spoiler from *Survivor: The Australian Outback*. This poster came on and claimed to have obtained inside info from his uncle, a CBS cameraman working on the show. He started predicting boot order of the contestants and got the first one right, and then a second one, and then another, and then…everything went totally wrong. The spoiler disappeared, without a trace of an explanation. It was the kind of experience that left the spoiler community understandably suspicious.

But as soon as this accusation began to take shape, black light poster, one of my earliest and most consistent supporters, shot it down. While admitting that it certainly was at least theoretically possible that I could be an insider, black light said that "my ubergut tells me ChillOne is legit and not part of a company scam."

Still, I could see that the doubters were circling my thread like buzzards. At the same time, other posters were picking up on the cast info I did reveal and were already speculating about whether the men and women I described might be the first four boots or even the Final 4. Also, CBS suddenly and "unexpectedly" revealed *Survivor: The Amazon* cast names, along with photos and some bio info, on their website. That was advance information, coming ahead of their scheduled unveiling of the all contestants on *The Early Show* on TV on Monday morning, the 13th. Could CBS be moving forward because of my intel? I had to wonder. In any event, their info helped the SurvivorSucks crowd match up names to my descriptions: Christy was the deaf girl, Daniel was the Asian guy, Brian was really Ryan, and Joanna was the African-American female.

So with all this new information out there, I knew I simply could not hold back my primary intel any longer. In my post at 2:42 p.m. that Saturday, I unveiled my boot order and Final 4, as told to me during that night-time rendez-vous with Enrique and my boat driver in the Ariau bar:

"*PECKING ORDER:*

With the honor of being voted off 1ˢᵗ (drum roll please)…

Daniel

Followed by:

Ryan (not Brian), Joanna (African American contestant), and 'Another lady around 30'

FINAL 4 (2W, 2M):

Deaf Girl (as previously mentioned)

Jana or Jenna, 23

Another guy, 26; "strong build"

Another guy, 50

Now, we have some noticeable "gaps", and this is where I'm relying on this forum to help put the puzzle together. As I mentioned earlier, I did not push for names…I was more interested in trying to see filming locations.

Some notes (to help with the name-game puzzle):

* I was told that 'Jana or Jenna, 23', was not the most "attractive" girl coming into the show, but, at the end (being in the Final 4) and loosing sound lb.'s, this contestant was considered to be the best looking. Now, that puts a little twist on my information. Jenna M. is a hottie coming into the show (based on the pics), so, maybe my sources were thinking of Jeanne Herbert (who looks more "average, all-American girl" sized vs. the thin model type)???Hmmmmm…Then again, maybe Jenna M. was a few pounds heavier coming into the show (beefed-up knowing the food situation would be scarce). Anyway, I will go with Jenna M. for the Final 4.

* The 'Another guy, 26: "strong build" was how this contestant was described to me. My sources forgot the name. Maybe its Alex, or Dave, or Matthew. I was told this person had a "tight" haircut possibly parted on the side. Also, this person was described as "big" from a muscle perspective. Not body fat. This person also lost some major lb.'s.

* The 'Another guy, 50' could be either Roger or Butch. I will lean toward Roger since my sources did not mention a mustache.

Now, as more information is uncovered, we (as a spoiler team) should be able to build a better F4 off this skeleton. I am sorry this is all I can provide, but at least its something to work with.

Please let me know if you have any questions…

—The ChillOne"

Again, I was playing with the community by underplaying the significance of what I was unveiling. It was just a "skeleton," I said. The truth was that no one had ever entered the spoiling community several weeks before any *Survivor* season had begun and given such specific information about who goes early and who is still around at the end. With this post, I was simply trying to enhance the buzz I already had stirred, and to coax the SurvivorSucks spoilers into coming back asking for more intel. I could see them plunging right into figuring out what my intel meant and trying to fill in the cracks, and the questions they asked were keeping me pumped up. I had them hooked from the start. It was all going exactly as planned.

Of course, there were those cracks. When my boat driver had told me that a 50-year-old man makes the Final 4, I had assumed there would be only one male that old in the cast. But Butch and Roger were both about that age. With no other clarifying info from my source, I realized that this part of the puzzle could remain unsolved for awhile. Then, there was that matter of the big, strong 26-year-old Final 2 male. I was studying the male contestants carefully from the CBS list, while thinking back to just how my source had described him. I felt I was getting closer and closer to pinning this person down as that Saturday wore on.

First, it was time to zero in on my Final 4. In my main post earlier that day, I had simply given my source's descriptions of the Final 4 without saying anything about order within that grouping. I was still teasing, leading them on. At 7:34 p.m., I added that critical piece of intel:

"Well, The ChillOne is not done yet…further intel tells me that:

4th place: Deaf girl

3rd place: Roger or Butch which leaves Jenna and either Alex, Dave, or Matthew as the Sole Survivor Intel tells me that Jenna was "liked" more than her final 2 competitor (whichever dude that may be). But, we all know how that final episode can go…"

So now I had made my Final 2 public, for the record. And I dangled a tantalizing clue as to who the Sole Survivor MIGHT be. I felt totally revved. But in my over-eagerness, I then made one strategic mistake. In the name of further establishing my Joe Tourist identity, I decided to post a photo of myself on the thread. Oops. Shortly after posting that photo, I realized that some very savvy computer person might be able to take that photo and determine my real name and other basic info from the underlying file properties. Blowing my cover in this way would be a way of spoiling the spoiler. Besides, hiding my true identity would make ChillOne, and my story, all the more intriguing. So I quickly pulled my photo off-line. Fortunately for me, only a handful of people saw it and no one spread it. I was safe, but I had flirted with potential disaster.

As a comeback, I went on the board with my interpretation of my Final 2 male. At 9:07 p.m., I revealed:

"*For some reason I keep going back to Matthew (even though he's older than 26).*"

Boom! There it was. A Final 4, the names of the Final 2, a tip about who was better liked of the two finalists. And it was all out there a full month before the February 13 first episode. In those first two days of my thread, I had attracted 340 posts! The reputation of ChillOne, and the debates about his intel, were off to a roaring start.

5

THE SPOILER ROOM HEATS UP

The postings on ChillOne's thread continued to roll in at an amazing pace. Everyone wanted to give his or her opinion on ChillOne's intel and who he really was. And if one person's opinion got ripped by someone else, that first person would come back to defend their position with fury and flair. I tried to keep up with it all, but the postings just kept flying practically through the night. Probably, some posters lived in the West in the later time zone. But it also looked as if some of these people who flock to the spoiler rooms apparently just don't go to bed very early, if at all.

When I got to work and checked my thread on Monday morning, January 13th, I studied all the activity since I had turned in on Sunday night and made this posting at 7:02 a.m.:

"WOW…I mean, WOW. I go to bed, wake-up, come into work, check the board, and BOOM. Man, my head is spinning right now."

An hour later, black light poster advised me that "it's gonna be a long ride, you ain't seen nothin yet, ChillOne."

Black light was dead right about that. I knew I had to fasten my seat belt for this wild ride. In that first full week after my initial January 9th posting, my thread recorded 680 total posts. And that was still four weeks before the first episode of *Survivor: The Amazon*! In the entire period from January 9 until the kick-off show on February 13, it seemed as if every conceivable idea and possibility was tossed into the mixing pot for consideration, or just to get under somebody's skin—usually mine.

I witnessed all kinds of conspiracy theories. We had open alliances, hinted alliances, and accused alliances. We had attacks and counter-attacks. We had people threatening to bolt and people threatened with expulsion. We had arguments about the pronunciation of certain letters in Portuguese, and arguments about whether Canadians typically pronounce and spell a common word wrong. We had discussions about naked breasts and debates about breast implants and which female *Survivor* cast members had them. We had outlines of merges and fake merges. We had speculation about true evidence, false evidence, and planted evidence.

Basically, we had everything that makes any Internet forum lively, with some of the same ingredients that also make *Survivor* a great TV show. And I found myself right in the center of the storm. I was the main subject of this reality "game" about a reality TV game. The questions about who I really was and the accusations that I was a hoax or a plant cropped up practically every day. For example, on January 12th Jedijake posted at 9:46 p.m.:

"We are indebted to your facts, Chill. However, I think you are more on the inside than we'd like to think."

Three minutes later, I shot back:

"As I mentioned, NONE of my information came from CBS or SEG (Survivor Entertainment Group)*...NONE, NONE, NONE."*

Of course, my attempts to put an end to the rumors of being a plant didn't stop them from coming. Sometimes, it just seemed to fuel the fire. The most frequent charge was that I was an insider orchestrated by the staff of CBS or SEG. That theory mostly speculated that my intel would prove relatively accurate in the beginning so that people would believe my Final 4 information, but that this later information was deliberately planted as false. That way, no one would really know which contestants made it that far and who won.

Many in the spoiler room community found some credibility in this theory because the Final 2 of *Survivor 5* was known weeks before the show actually revealed Clay and Brian as the last two survivors. The spoiler site TrueDork-Times reported this news about three weeks before the final episode, and SurvivorSucks and others picked up on it. At the time, it didn't seem possible because Clay was being shown as a lazy, hotheaded redneck. But, of course, it proved to be right on the mark. So now the spoiler community wondered if CBS was trying to head off any real leaks about who wins *Survivor 6* by laying a false trail to a totally inaccurate Final 4. And ChillOne, according to this theory, was the willing conduit of this devious CBS maneuver.

Ouch. I knew that questioning the messenger would be part of the deal, but I still had hoped that the jury of the spoiler room would soon enough come to the conclusion that I was telling the truth. I had hoped they would invest all their time, energy, and wisdom into helping to solve the missing pieces of my puzzle. I had some non-specific items that needed to be deciphered, such as the real identity of the 26-year-old big male in the Final 2 and the 50-year-old male in the Final 4, and I wanted them to work along with me to do it. But that was one wish that clearly was not going to come true.

So even as the heat got turned up, I mostly stuck to my plan. I addressed just about every question posed to me and tried to be honest with them. I just had to tell the truth and let my intel run its course, even though it was going to be a long time before the episodes starting playing out on CBS. In the mean time, they could believe what they wanted.

Some believed in some very strange theories. At one point I was accused of coming up with all my contestant information from getting a look at an early copy of the *TV Guide* issue that previewed *Survivor: The Amazon*. I was also accused of living in Canada because I spelled the word "lose" as "loose" when referring to Jenna losing weight, and supposedly Canadians do that frequently. That theory went on that if I really lived in Canada instead of Boston as I had revealed, I must be lying about everything else! Another critic dissected my posting name and pointed out that the initials CO for ChillOne were the first two letters of Communist. I also got accused of making up all my intel just to get attention.

Then again, I also had my supporters. Black light poster, despite doubts, was someone who took my intel seriously and diligently tried to work with it. A prolific poster named Orangeena also rallied behind me while diving into my clues to figure out how the contestants would wind up in the results my intel pointed toward. She also acknowledged me for my patience, especially in a post on January 21st at 6:15 p.m.:

"You must be the most patient poster in the world. You answer everyone's questions so even-handedly."

Less than a week later, Dan Bollinger also stood up for me against the most chronic critics of the board:

"Geez Lueez, folks! First you condemn CO because he didn't post everything fast enough; then because he should have given out the information slowly. Now because he posted more than a newbie oughta. There's legit complaints and there's complaining, and then there's bitching. Is that sour grapes I'm smelling?"

Yes, the complainers made a lot of noise. And my supporters scored some good counterpoints. But the more I studied all the activity on my SurvivorSucks thread, the more I could see that there were all kinds of different characters playing this game. When I stopped to look at their personalities more closely, I saw them fitting into these general categories:

The Believers: Many posters just took my intel as being quite true and tried to analyze the cast information and previews from CBS to figure out how my first four boots could pan out, or how my Final 4 could survive all that way through the season. Again, Orangeena was especially adept at this. Orangeena even deducted in the first week of my thread that my primary source was an Ariau boat driver, though I did not specifically say so. I had been dropping hints, hoping that someone would figure it out because so many questions were being raised about how I could have obtained such important intel. Orangeena was the one to nail it.

Orangeena also concluded for herself, from studying *Survivor 6* cast photos and remembering back to trends from past *Survivor* seasons, that Jenna and Matt really would be the Final 2. Orangeena did that way back on January 16th, only days after I had shared that as part of my intel. Having such a diligent and respected poster using logic to come to a conclusion that validated my intel was a big boost for me.

Within this category of believers, I also saw a distinction between the hard-core believers and the skeptical believers. The hard-core believers are the kind of supporters who might jump in and take bullets for you when the heat got intense. The skeptical believers had reservations about my intel. They seemed to want to believe while wanting to keep an open mind.

The Non-Believers: This group seemed never to accept that my intel had any merit and that I was even who I said I was. To them, I simply could not be a tourist who used the basic techniques of undercover operations to take advantage of a situation I just happened to find myself in when I got to the Amazon.

Posters in this category also seemed to come in different flavors. Some non-believers were kind and friendly in their attitude toward me, even while they raised objections about my intel and poked at what they saw as holes in my conclusions. Other non-believers were more prone to personal attacks. They were the kind you just didn't want to meet out on the street, or on the board. In Internet lingo, these kinds of characters are instantly recognized as:

The Flamers. Even flamers could be further broken down. Some I would call the extreme flamers, those who attack and attack until they get a reaction from you. They sometimes resort to the kind of vulgarity that is supposed to be prohibited on ezboard. Others I would call intellectual flamers, those who insult you using seemingly wise and reasoned arguments.

The Lurkers: These are the people who enjoy the thread and probably don't want it to die but seldom come on to post anything themselves. They pop in for one or two posts, or a very short series of posts, and then just disappear. These people could be harmless, simply choosing to come on when they felt extremely motivated or angered by one point on the thread. But my spying instincts told me I had to be careful of these lurkers. They actually could be characters who best fit another category:

The Double Spoilers: These are the people who could be operating as "double agents" within the spoiling community by appearing under two or more different posting aliases. They come on with the different posting name to test out a position they don't want associated with their main alias or to make a jab they don't want to be held accountable for.

But a double spoiler could be even more dangerous. They could be CBS plants who come on to sabotage or deceive. I didn't know for sure whether any of the posters on my thread actually did work for CBS, but like most posters I did believe it was possible. I suspect that CBS at least monitors SurvivorSucks and other spoiler sites, and it seemed a viable possibility that they flush out the potential spoilers like mine and post on the board to create confusion.

From early on, I certainly believed that my spoiler did at least force CBS to make strategic decisions about *Survivor 6*. What I did in naming details of game dynamics and pointing to a Final 4, a Final 2, and a possible winner so long before a *Survivor* season had even begun was totally unprecedented. Maybe it prompted them to call some kind of emergency meeting to develop a strategy to combat my intel and its impact. Throwing up cast photos and bios on their website on the weekend of January 10-12 might have been one example of such a strategy.

CBS also knows that the spoiling community attracts hundreds or even thousands of *Survivor*'s most devoted fans. More important, major breakthrough information in the spoiling room often attracts major news media. And if the media steps in and "spoils" the results of the show before it airs, that could be seen as a potential ratings threat. Many people may not want to watch a reality TV program like *Survivor* if they know how it's going to turn out. Although I certainly cannot prove any CBS response maneuver to my spoiler, I believe it happened.

Still, while I sometimes wondered about CBS lurking about, and I made note of all these other kinds of characters on my thread, my instincts told me not to get involved in a tug of war in my mind about who was who and what it meant. I determined that a more effective strategy would be to break down the spoiler room cast into three basic groups: Supporters, Flamers, and the Administrator. To put it another way: the good guys, the bad guys, and the ref or judge.

That simplified my strategy. I did whatever I could to help our side, the good guys, be heard more. I did whatever I could to get the bad guys boxed into a position of being told to shut up. One weapon that worked like a charm was to demand that they prove their accusations about me, which of course they couldn't do. Other times the best strategy was to let my hard-core supporters rebut the flamer. I was often not only appreciative but extremely impressed by how well they did that. Also, when my supporters responded to the critics, it allowed me to stay above the fray, something any smart *Survivor* contestant would try to do. The last part of my strategy was to make sure the "judge" didn't see enough evidence to want to "lock" my thread. That would be like a survivor having his or her torch extinguished, and I was determined that this was not going to happen to me. I was going to be the sole survivor in the spoiler room.

Sometimes I tried to derail the flamers and non-believers before they got much steam going. On January 18th, I sharply rebutted a poster named Thebes, who was building some case about the timing of my intel about the Final 4 pecking order and Final 2. After pointing out that I outlined my primary intel on January 10th before adding the Final 4 the next day, I added:

"Can you please explain to me why you think it's such a big deal with my decision of posting my pecking order, F4, and F2 a day later???

Ahhhh…anyway, whatever. It doesn't matter.

My information is out there. Read into it as much as you like.…Poke holes in that which you desire. Pat me on the back as you see fit. This is all fine by me. I heard what I heard."

The truth was, Thebes got under my skin a little. But my strategy worked. She soon came on and admitted to being an old bitter skeptic and cooled on the accusation. Others were not so easy to chase away. But often that was fine. I found many of their theories merely entertaining and I understood that they had a right to try to test my intel. As non-believer JackOfSpeed posted on January 14th at 9:47 a.m.:

"I am just trying to move things forward in a positive direction and weed out the background noise. If that means holding ChillOne's feet to the fire over some inconsistencies than so be it."

I must admit that I did display a few inconsistencies. From the outset, I knew that being a reliable informant meant not getting too caught up in speculation. I should just stick to the information that I picked up from my sources. Back my intel, let the others speculate. Well, my source identified Jenna as the female who makes the F2 and even was better liked than her male counterpart there. But some posters on my thread turned away from this part of my intel and substituted theories about the "J" sound in Portuguese sounding like the "Sh" sound. To them, this meant that my source really was saying "Shawna" instead of Jenna when referring to the female contestant in the F2. These posters figured that Shawna was actually a more likely fit for the F2 anyway because it was hard to believe that Jenna, the model, only became attractive as the game wore on.

For a few days, I engaged in this speculation with them. I even strongly suggested that Shawna could be the F2 female my source was trying to identify. But then I began to analyze this theory more closely behind the scenes. I accepted the speculation about Shawna as a valid argument, but I kept going back to the Ariau bar on that pivotal evening of intel gathering. I kept revisiting how Enrique pronounced Jenna. Was there a soft "J" sound? Maybe, but *very slight*. Then I looked at the white piece of paper that I brought back from the Amazon, the one Enrique used to write down my source's Final 4. All signs pointed to Jenna, not Shawna. Before long, I corrected myself on the board. The young woman in the Final 2 was Jenna. Period. I tried to put this controversy to rest.

Around this same time, I decided to make another bold maneuver in my undercover role. I knew that the one person who could clear up this Jenna/ Shawna debate, and the arguments about which cast member really fit the big, strong, 26-year-old male description as the other slot in the F2, was my source back at the Ariau. But how could I possibly contact that boat driver? It would have to be done through Enrique of course, but I was in no position to make a return trip to the Amazon. But what about email? Even in the Amazon, it was quite possible that Enrique had an email address, and a good agent ought to be able to obtain it.

And so I did. I contacted the Miami-based headquarters of the Ariau and told them via an email letter that I had enjoyed a wonderful time there in early January. I praised the entire Ariau staff for their hospitality and personally mentioned Enrique as a great jungle guide. That was all true enough, of course, but I was using this praise only as a cover for my real mission. I told them that I had a photo of Enrique that I wanted to send to him and wondered if they had an email address for him. Without asking me a single question, they gave it to me.

Knowing that this would likely be my last contact with my source, I decided to shoot for the works. I sent Enrique a full *Survivor 6* cast photo and asked him to approach the boat driver to clear up some confusion that I had regarding what he had told me. I asked him to point out the Final 2 female named Jana or Jenna, the F2 male with the big, strong build, and the 50-year-old male in the Final 4. I even asked him to point to each person in the photo and give me their order in being voted off. If I obtained all this information, my new intel would blow everyone in the spoiler community totally away!

At first, I got no response from Enrique at all. Then, a little more than a week after my email, he finally replied. His email explained that he didn't respond right away because the Internet at the Ariau was down again and he only checked his email when he got back to Manaus. He told me he would bring the photos back to the Ariau and try to get answers from the boat driver for me.

I never heard from him again. Did something or someone stop him? Did CBS or SEG trace the origin of their leak? Did they make a phone call to the Ariau owners? Did my boat driver get fired? Was my email to Enrique, or any response he might have tried to send me, intercepted? I could only wonder, and to hope for the best for my trusted sources.

Some of my thread's believers speculated that CBS and Ariau management were all in an uproar over how some tourist like me could have infiltrated the secrets of *Survivor*. Well, even if no one got fired I certainly could imagine CBS wanting to take steps to make sure something like this didn't happen again. Of course, others in the spoiler room speculated that instead of causing problems for CBS my intel might actually make them happy by jazzing the ratings of *Survivor: The Amazon*. Why? People who had heard about ChillOne would tune in to see if I was right, and if so how it could work out that way. I didn't know about that. I only knew that I would be watching every episode very, very closely myself.

By February 6th, the first episode was only a week away. I was anxious to see what would happen but confident in my intel. I was hoping for 100% accuracy, though I recognized that my boat driver might not have remembered such details as the early boot order that clearly. Still, in responding to another accusation of my being a hoax, I put up this post:

"If things do not play out as documented (by me) in this thread…it will just go down, in my mind, as misreported information, NOT A HOAX. I'm just an "Average Joe" who happened to be in the right place at the right time. Things just fell on my lap. Consider me a conduit, not a conspirator.

That is all. One week and counting…"

By that point, SurvivorSucks had become my primary focus in life. I still maintained my day job, and I didn't give up my early-evening workouts at the gym. But after I got home, I got right down to business, starting with slipping my Healthy Choice dinner into the microwave. As a follower of the Bill Phillips *Body for Life* program, I eat six small meals a day, following my routine like a robot. My choice of dinner meant no wasted time for cooking or cleaning, as well as portion control on my plan. Then, zoom, it was time to get to the Internet. I would scan all the posts and then begin to craft my reply with two windows open, the one I would be typing in and the other the post I was reading to cut and paste excerpts of questions from posters. I'd continue this process late into the night, and then have my sixth meal before bed.

I would arrive at work very early every morning and, after taking care of any pressing work issues in my email box, I'd scan the overnight SurvivorSucks posts before starting my full-scale work day. On weekends, I was pumped to have most of my time to devote to my thread. Gone was all that time I used to spend watching other reality TV shows. I even gave up my weekly poker night with the guys. These days, the game on my thread was the only one that mattered. An experienced agent always keeps an ever watchful eye over the fate of his intel.

After my February 6ᵗʰ post, I thought the thread would stay pretty quiet in those final days before Ep.1 (spoiler room abbreviation for episode numbers of a *Survivor* season). But I didn't count on the arrival of a pesky new poster named Intelly. An admitted newbie, Intelly insisted from his entry late in our spoiling game that I go back over many details that had been referred to over and over again. I politely referred Intelly to my previous posts, which only seemed to fan the flames. On February 7ᵗʰ Intelly made this post at 2:42 p.m.:

"Why no personality ChillONE?…Do you tell your friends refer to my conversation last week?"

That was only the beginning. Intelly continued to piss me off. "BE A MAN NOT A ROBOT," he wrote in another post. And Intelly practically demanded that I tell the board everything I had done on my Amazon vacation. The absence of such references to this poster proved that I "was not there." Just because I did not refer to specific kinds of bugs found in the Amazon, my whole vacation must have been formed from text and photos, just a bunch of fiction. *Arggggghhhh.*

But that wasn't enough. Intelly then took to re-posting many of my previous posts on the thread in a non-stop campaign to blow the lid off my intel. That tactic bogged down the thread and infuriated many of the believers, many of whom stood up as hard-core supporters and told Intelly to get off my back. In response, Intelly just accused those supporters of being in cahoots with me, or even of being other aliases that I was speaking through myself. The clear implication was that I wasn't able to stand up for myself.

That was enough for me. I knew this sort of thing, left unchecked, could potentially undermine my thread. Anyway, I was boiling. So on February 9ᵗʰ I made this 10:34 p.m. post:

"This is what's called a Survivor message forum, not The Travel Channel…Who the hell are you to tell me what my vacation was formed upon…Dude, you are one strange mo-fo. You are officially 'dead-to-me.'"

In the world of postings on Internet forums, this was as strong a declaration as you could make that, all kidding aside, you weren't going to take what someone was throwing at you anymore. Picture James Bond resorting to a sophisticated fist-fight when cornered by the bad guys.

I was making a statement that while I would keep my commitment to answer question after question posed to me related to my intel, I had my limits. I would not treat with respect someone who was simply trying to goad and insult me. I was standing by my intel and would not be chased away. As *Survivor 6* drew close to launching time, I was sitting firmly in the capsule, all seat belts securely fastened…waiting for liftoff.

6

LET THE GAME BEGIN

Two days before the first episode of *Survivor: The Amazon*, ChillOne scored his first national exposure outside the Internet. Michael Hewitt, who writes about reality TV shows in his column in *The Orange County Register*, had contacted me and asked for a brief interview. I decided that gaining attention in the media would only strengthen my spoiling hand, so I quickly agreed. But when he asked me if he could use my real name, I declined. It was too important to maintain my cover. Fortunately, he agreed to refer to me as ChillOne in his column.

"Lately, the spoiling world has been buzzing over reports from a guy who calls himself ChillOne....The community now rages with debate over whether ChillOne has given them a gold mine or a land mine," this reporter wrote in the February 11 edition of *The Orange County Register*.

Now I was even more psyched for the real game of *Survivor: The Amazon* to get going. More and more people knew about my intel and would be watching the season closely to see how it came out. Even with the flamers to fight off, I was having more and more fun on the SurvivorSucks board. I got a good laugh when Antithesys came up with the name Uncle Boat Driver to refer to my primary source and, by extension, also to me. This was a spin-off of the name Uncle Camerman, the most notorious spoiler from *Survivor 2*, so it had a real spoiler ring to it. It also gave my source more character. Privately, I even began to think of my Brazilian source as Uncle Boat Driver, although on the board itself I still referred to him as "my source." I wanted to maintain the proper demeanor of an informant.

I faced another test of my ability to exercise restraint and keep my cover before the first episode. When one poster lightheartedly tossed in still another conspiracy theory, this one suggesting that I was a spy for the NSA stationed off Nova Scotia, I didn't respond at all. I could have revealed the irony of his accusation as it related to one of my many past professional work experiences, but I refrained. I was willing to reveal what I did for a living and the extent of my international travel, but some details of my past would need to remain off the board.

I did take one last opportunity before Ep.1 to stand up to another personal attack. Just after responding to Intelly's nonsense, I noticed the accusations and insults escalating from JackOfSpeed. When he called me "a loser," I shot back, "…a little uncalled for, don't you think?" JOS was crossing the line even further by swearing like a truck driver. Then, when he compared me to a cheating golfer with some references to the timing of my release of my intel, I pointed out that I had spoiled the information about the deaf contestant and the gender tribal split before any media or magazine confirmation. "That, my friend, can be considered a hole-in-1," I wrote.

Standing up firmly to this flamer inspired a new poster named atruequeen to post:

"I am just glad that you have been a big enough person to take the beating you have been getting as this has been the most exciting thing related to Survivor in a while and has me really excited about this season."

That post was a typical example of how my strategy in responding to criticism helped me to gain more support on my thread. And when new supporters jumped in to defend me, I was able to sit back and let the flamer take the heat. Of course, I knew that I hadn't seen the last of the flamers. As *Survivor: The Amazon* began, I knew they would be studying every development, ready to pounce on any part of my intel that did not turn out to be accurate so that they could start the fires burning. So the flamers were watching. My supporters were watching. And I was watching. As the much-anticipated evening of February 13th arrived, all we could do was wait. As Dan Bollinger put it in his post at 7:23 p.m.:

"It is 7:30 and it suddenly got very quiet in here, after three months of shouting… We've cussed and discussed just about everything. I'm off to shower, put on some sweats, warm the couch, tune into CBS, and open a pint of Ben & Jerry's."

Ep.1: "Boys vs. Girls"—Well, Daniel was not the first boot. When the vote was announced and Ryan became the first to be voted off *Survivor,* I knew I would take my lumps on the board for having my first predicted boot wrong. But both Ryan AND Daniel stumbled on the balance beam during the Immunity Challenge and cost the men victory there. That was totally consistent with what my source had said.

More important, I liked what I saw in this first action look at my predicted Final 4 contestants, especially Matt and Jenna. Neither of them were doing anything stupid—none of the kinds of mistakes that could leave them vulnerable to an early boot. Both seemed to be flying below the radar. At this early juncture, I liked their chances.

As I turned to SurvivorSucks after the program, I decided that I needed to post right away. I had always said that I would admit when I was wrong. If I jumped on and acknowledged my intel error in an honest and graceful manner, I would take a huge step in gaining integrity. So at 9:54 p.m., I posted:

"Greetings…

Well, what can I say. Daniel did not go first. I will certainly mark it down and admit to being incorrect.

On another note, congrats to all who worked to unravel the vid caps and isolate Ryan as the first boot. Good job. You all deserve a pat on the back.

Now, for all of you who are thinking ahead to Episode 2…

No, I do not feel any less confident in my information. I will just chalk up tonight's vote to my source getting Ryan and Daniel's boot order mixed up. I will still hold to my intel that the women will again win immunity in Episode 2. Additionally, I believe that it was just a brain-flop on the part of my source and back Daniel being the second voted off next week.

AGAIN…it is very important to note that a great majority of my Survivor conversations focused on the F4, not the initial boot order. So, with that in mind, I think some very positive things came out of tonight episode…

* Butch (in my mind) is now looking better-than-ever as our older F4 male participant. Roger has rubbed people the wrong way in just 3 days. I cannot see him recovering. Butch to the F4 to join Christy.

* I also believe that Matthew is the other F4/F2 male. Dude is jacked-up. He is the only one (again, in my mind) that fits the description as described by my source.

A few other notes…

* When Joanna and the other chick went out fishing, did you guys notice the white sandy beach in the background??? Well, I'm pretty sure that that place was the "back-side" of Challenge Beach as outlined by Dan. I have pictures of the area pointing out toward the water where Joanna and the other girl were fishing.

* Did anyone notice the 2 wooden figures that Matt (I believe) pulled out of the tree-mail. Well, it just so happens that I have the exact same one in my living room…bought it at the souvenir shop at the Ariau.

Well, I'm tuning in for the night. Again, I will be happy to answer your questions (if you have any at this point).

—The ChillOne"

I felt totally satisfied with this post. I admitted I was wrong, pointed out where I was right, and congratulated those who had correctly predicted Ryan to get the first boot. I also demonstrated my consistency by vowing to respond to all questions, just as I had been doing from the start. Also, I had now officially put names to every member of the Final 4 as outlined by Uncle Boat Driver in the Amazon. When my source had said that a 50-year-old male reached the Final 4, I assumed the name would become obvious from the cast list. But when both Roger and Butch fit the age range, I had no other clues from my source to draw upon and was left to speculate to pin down this contestant. I felt pleased now that I could definitively name Butch after only one episode.

Part of my strategy with this post was to make a pre-emptive strike against the non-believers. By admitting to being wrong, while also pointing out where I was clearly right and inviting everyone to shift their attention to the future, I was hoping to avoid a week's worth of attacks. As that first long night after Ep.1 dragged on, my strategy appeared to be working. Most of the posters shrugged off my inaccurate boot because my intel had tabbed Ryan as the second boot and Daniel appeared very vulnerable to being off voted off in Ep.2. So it certainly looked like I was on the right path. Instead of tearing me apart, most spoilers got back to looking for clues and analyzing what they had seen on the show. In other words, they got back to spoiling *Survivor* instead of trying to spoil the spoiler (me).

When I woke up the next morning, I was especially gratified and surprised to see this post from JackOfSpeed at 9:12 a.m.:

"ChillOne, sorry that your intel didn't pan out in the 1ˢᵗ episode. I hope it gets better from here on out, but I don't think it will. Regardless of the questioning/heckling I have given you, I am a spoiler by nature, and was secretly hoping somebody had finally stumbled upon the Holy Grail of EPM"

Wow, no nasty "I told you so" remarks! I took this as an opening to try to recruit JOS over to the good guys, perhaps as a skeptical believer who would work the clues of my intel with us. I responded to him in the same tone as his post:

"Hey, some of it (my intel) did!!! Anyway, we'll have to see how it all plays out. I'm just as anxious as everyone else out here. And, as far as the Holy Grail…IMHO, my F4 is still alive and kickin'. We just need to work to fill in some of the spoiler gaps (which I think will happen very soon…by watching the first few episodes things might become much clearer).
—The ChillOne"

The funny thing about my morning post is that on the header, right under my alias, the usual term of "Registered User" had been stripped away. In its place, the Administrator had substituted the tag "Soon to be banned." A little Survivor-

Sucks humor there, I figured. No way ChillOne was going to be banned. Without being cocky, I knew that my thread was the best thing to happen to the site in a very long time. Many of the regulars said so. The thread had just been featured in a major newspaper article, and SurvivorSucks had become Central Command of the spoiling season, with more traffic coming to their site because of my thread than ever before. People were visiting from competing spoiler sites just to view my posts, and those other sites were beginning to make more and more mention of SurvivorSucks.

So SurvivorSucks had far too much going for it to "lock" my thread because I missed the Daniel boot. Plus, I still had *so* much more out there: the next three boots, the nudity scene, the Final 4, the Final 2. Until all of that was debunked, my spoiler would remain very much alive. Anyway, even if SurvivorSucks did lock my thread down, it would cause quite an uprising on the board. And I would just take my intel and move on. Like any seasoned informant, I kept open a contingency plan in case of a development like that. Already, I had received many invitations to join other groups, forums, or spoiler sites. One way or another, my intel would survive and remain public while *Survivor: The Amazon* went on.

Still, I was keeping close tabs on any trends or shifts on my thread. I wanted THIS thread on THIS board to stand up for the entire season. So it was a bit disturbing on the evening of February 14th when Jedijake, who admittedly had been playing both the role of supporter and skeptic in previous posts, came out and charged again that I was working hand-in-hand with CBS. In trying to substantiate this charge, he drew a comparison to the famous Gervase X "spoiler" of the very first *Survivor* season.

That one still struck a raw nerve in the spoiling world. The Gervase X "spoiler" centered on one of the contestants, a man by the name of Gervase Petersen. An Internet coding savvy poster by the name of CAP LOCK claimed to have hacked into the CBS.com website and uncovered photos of 15 survivors with red X's in the corner. Remember, *Survivor* begins with 16 contestants. After each episode, CBS was posting a red X over the picture of the contestant voted off that week. So, all the red X's were there, in code, but not visible to the general web surfer who visited the CBS.com *Survivor* site.

The theory was that the CBS.com analysts had pre-coded the red X's over the 15 contestants to make their programming life easier when each week's contestant was voted off. Only one person, Gervase, lacked an X. From this "clue," CAP LOCK concluded that Gervase had to be the winner of the season, and CBS had screwed up big time by leaving a trail to follow. There was a precedent of sorts, as the spoilers viewed it. CBS webmasters had accidentally posted the summary for Episode 8 hours before it aired.

The Gervase X revelation made national headlines and transformed Survivor-Sucks from obscurity to cult status. The official word from CBS: "No comment." Meanwhile, more and more people lined up behind this "spoiler." Speculation was rampant that Gervase would be the inaugural season's Sole Survivor. Instead, he was voted off in Ep.10, finishing in seventh place. So Gervase X became the first of many spoilers gone wrong that left SurvivorSucks and all of the spoiling community suspicious of new attempts to nail the winner or Final 2 early on. Like many other spoilers, I had to believe that CAP LOCK was a CBS plant with the prime motive of hoaxing the spoiling community into thinking that Gervase would become the Sole Survivor. So I could understand the spoilers initially reacting to my thread with a nervous eye toward CBS.

But in this latest round of the debate about my spoiler, the non-believers weren't winning many converts against me. Most posters were taking a wait-and-see approach before making absolute judgments about my intel. And again, I picked up new votes among the more silent segment of the crowd, as evidenced by this post from nisi2u at 10:02 a.m. on February 16th:

"All I know is ChillOne sucked me in hook line and sinker for this season just in order to see if what he's told us is the truth. Whether or not he's right on the majority…doesn't matter because I had totally lost interest in the damned show during Africa…I haven't been this pumped about a season since 2. Kudos' to him for reviving it. Brilliant!!!!!"

I was always thankful for new showings of support, but I wanted to see what followed it. In this situation, Orangeena stepped in to offer a second vote of confidence:

"C1 has totally put a much-needed shot of adrenaline into this tiring franchise!

At first I was very upset about having the whole season spoiled, but now it's become like a SECOND Survivor game to figure out. Just when is C1 (right)*, and when is he wrong."*

I totally agreed with Orangeena's perspective. Now that *Survivor: The Amazon* was underway, the spoiling community looked as if it would stay hooked on the habit of trying to guess when my intel would stand up and when it might get shot down. Posters were coming on just to predict what would happen on the show directly as it pertained to what I predicted and keeping scorecards of how well they were doing. Of course, our game also had the added twist of wondering whether more inaccurate boots from my intel might really confirm that I was a plant of EPMB (Evil Pecker Mark Burnett, another nickname frequently used for him in the spoiling world).

I was glad to see all this lively involvement. It kept my primary mission intact: to keep my thread alive for the entire season and eventually earn my way to Monster Island, sort of a Hall of Fame for any SurvivorSucks thread that stood out for the long haul and deserved preservation.

"So let them play this game," I said to myself. "They are interested. They are engaged. This is good."

It was also encouraging to see new posters joining the game and the debate. That helped ensure that my thread didn't become dominated by the regulars and turn others off. As Ep.2 approached, an infrequent poster named slimmyworm came in on the side of the supporters:

"Some of this stuff is probably going to be right, some of it is definitely going to be wrong—after all, we've already seen it happen. Doesn't mean ChillOne is screwing around with us. Discussing each minute detail of his earlier posts isn't really going to get us anywhere…"

Then TheIcemanPosteth signed on as a critic:

"In my mind, C1's info has lost its luster…C1's source can no longer be a lens through which all other evidence is scrutinized.

C1 has no interest in deceiving anyone. His sources suck. And those are the facts."

As the ongoing debate continued, I was still fascinated, and still hoping for the "good guys" to hold the upper hand or at least to keep things relatively even. But during the build-up to Ep.2, I was not all that concerned about the one wrong boot anyway. If anything, I probably felt more disappointed about some confusion that had cropped up during the week regarding Jenna and her weight. I knew that I had caused some of that confusion myself.

When I first reported my source as naming Jenna as the female in the Final 2, I noted that he described her as not being considered the most attractive female contestant early in the game but at the end, and after losing some pounds, she was considered the best looking. But I realized, and admitted to the board, that my source never actually said anything to me about Jenna's weight. I had simply speculated that losing weight was an important part of her becoming more attractive in the eyes of the men, so I threw that in.

However, as we all could see from Ep.1, the real reason Jenna was not considered the hottest female at the start of the season was because she did not flaunt herself to the men the way Heidi and Shawna did. With the tribes split by gender, she employed the strategy of not using her body and covering up as much as possible, especially with the way she wore her hair. Even when the women got together with the men in the early challenges, she played it conservative. As it turned out, this strategy would pay off handsomely for Jenna later.

For myself, I was reminded of the importance of not getting caught up in the temptation to mix in speculation in a way that detracted from my pure intel. That would risk confusion, and I wanted to keep all matters regarding my intel as clear as possible over these next 12 episodes. My success as a *Survivor* informant depended on it.

Copacabana, the world's most famous beach.

A small cross-section of Iguassu Falls.

The Com Te Souza (left) docked in Manaus.

Welcome to the jungle!

The Ariau Towers Hotel open-air lobby (at low water).

Tower #6 (back left), Ariau bar (back right), two fauna feeding stations (foreground).

"Thank you" plaque dedicated to the Ariau as referenced in Chapter 4 (Photo 1).

Challenge Beach as referenced in Chapter 4 (Photo 2).

Challenge Jungle location (on the banks of the Rio Ariau).

The path contestants walked as they approached/departed Tribal Council.

Tribal Council set location (voting station to the left, "bootee" exit to the right).

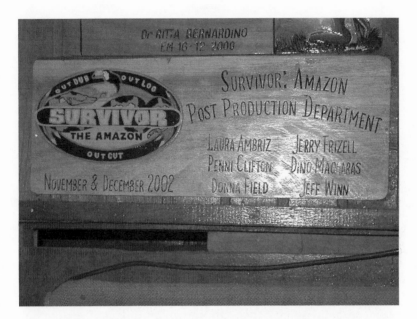

2nd plaque mounted in the Ariau's restaurant.

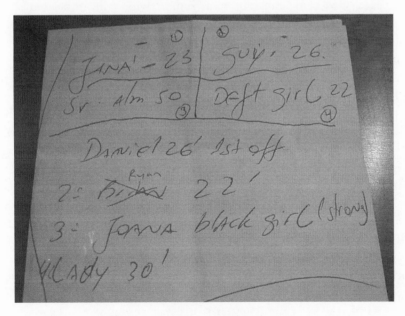

Contestant "intel" acquired at the Ariau.

7

A BOOT IN THE BUTT

"Storms," Ep.2 of *Survivor: The Amazon,* was about to begin. As I watched at home, I felt confident that Daniel would get the boot that night. If that happened, my intel for the first two boots would simply have been flip-flopped, with Ryan and Daniel out of order. The spoiling community would line up more strongly behind me, with the initial error almost forgotten. I'd be sailing along for the next couple of weeks, with the speculation about my Final 4 building and building. I was juiced at the prospect.

But a not-so-funny thing happened on the way to Daniel getting booted in Ep.2—Janet got voted off instead! I watched with dismay as Janet was shown to be sick, as well as being the subject of rumors within the tribe that she had sneaked in that granola bar. And with my intel's first four boots of Daniel, Ryan, Joanna, and a female about 30, Janet just did not fit the scorecard anywhere. She was much closer to 50 than 30.

Uh-oh. Personally, I could accept that my source simply didn't remember these first four boots very well. As I had cautioned the board, I got into much more detail with my source in discussing the Final 4 than these first four boots, and I knew it would have been much more difficult for him to remember back to these beginning episodes anyway. Also, Daniel and Joanna still looked extremely vulnerable, so if they did get voted off in the next couple of weeks it would mean that my overall intel for the first four boots, taken as a whole, would still be "in the ballpark." But the flamers, the non-believers, the skeptics, and maybe even a few believers were certainly going to "spin" this differently. I was prepared to get a swift kick in the butt. And I got it.

Before the evening of that second episode on February 20th had passed, the rumors of my being some kind of plant were becoming even more sinister on my SurvivorSucks thread. People were making further accusations about my concocting the photos from the Amazon that I had posted on the board. A non-believer named JayBerman insisted that many of my photos were "just still shots

58

found around the web using Google searches for beach shots and other people's vacation photos." Then a new poster named Behindthescenes came up with a theory that *Survivor: The Amazon* did not even have a post-production crew at the Ariau, meaning my photo of the plaque the crew left behind at the hotel had to have been totally fabricated!

While this trail of suspicion got dirtier and dirtier, SurvivorLover invited the board to participate in an immediate vote on my fate and the fate of my thread. The choices were: "1. Go to Monster Island; 2. Go to Purgatory; 3. Get locked and fade into obscurity…never to be heard from again." SurvivorLover kicked off the poll by voting for #3.

I still managed to get some decent sleep that night, but when I reviewed the overnight postings at work the next morning I knew I was looking at a very serious situation. Could the board really vote me off at this early juncture? I sure didn't think so, and if they did lock the thread it would be a huge mistake because my spoiler would still be talked about and referenced over and over until the Final 4 anyway. Still, the threat was out there. As I assessed it with the eye of an undercover agent, I knew that I simply couldn't predict all the variables. That meant that what I did next was critical to my thread's future.

I saw three choices:

Lay low for awhile and hope the dust would settle.

Admit my intel was wrong again while trying to get the board focused on the future, as I did after Ep.1.

Devise a response strategy worthy of a good agent and a masterful player in this game within the game.

Without hesitation, I chose option #3. It wasn't enough just to respond. I needed to employ real, carefully reasoned strategy. I would begin by admitting to my error, and I would do so with class. I'd directly address the question about authenticity of my photos in a way that would take a big step toward putting that rumor to bed. And I would take a covert approach in trying to re-rally the troops behind me, using some reverse logic. Instinctively, I knew how to make this move. So at 7:14 a.m., I posted:

"Again, I will admit to being wrong. I do not have a problem with that. Look, I came to this board with information that I thought you'd find interesting…just helping out in the spirit of this forum. What boggles me is that fact that so many of you are rooting for spoilers to be wrong…I ask, why are you here??? It doesn't make sense to me.

Anyway, I was in the Amazon. I did visit the Ariau. I did take the photos. They are authentic and were not "doctored" in any way. They are the "real-deal". If you'd like, I'd be happy to post all my photo's from the Amazon. I too visited an authentic Amazon village (not the same one from last night, but one nonetheless). Any interest???

About my intel…don't know what to say except that my source was wrong with the initial boot order. Was I given false information…I really do not think so. I will chalk it up to my source just being off base (in an honest way). Again, I feel that my source was extremely sincere and was not trying to lead me down a wrong path. If he did purposely do this, I fell for it hook-line-and-sinker. But, I do not think that was the case. I still look for the boots of Daniel, Joanna, and the 30 y.o. woman to happen (possibly in that order) sometime later in the show. I still think the Final 4 is alive and kicking…even though Christy got a few votes and was painted in a negative light a bit last night.

I cannot stress enough that I'm not here to deceive or hoax. I came to this board to provide information for this group to work with and debate.

ANTI: If you desire to lock this thread (I've seen a few votes for this), feel free to do so.

FELLOW "SPOILERS": If you would like me to go away, I can do that. Spoiling this show is not my life…I just wanted to help the cause of this forum.

That is all. Enjoy the weekend.

—The ChillOne"

So there it was. By offering to leave, I was challenging the board to demand that I stay. Notice my use of caps for FELLOW "SPOILERS." Already in the game, I was used to the naysayers coming in and insisting that I was lying and arguing that my thread should be locked. I knew that undercurrent would continue, at least until Ep.3. What I wanted to do was to get my supporters up and off their…chairs to combat this sentiment. Inside, I could still rally my own spirits by remembering that I had other invitations of Internet forums to share my intel if SurvivorSucks really did get swayed by the flamers and non-believers and lock me down. But I still welcomed that external support around me because I still wanted very much for this to remain my home base of operations. Yes, when the show was over, I wanted to wind up on Monster Island.

So I sat back and waited for the board to act. It didn't take long. Later that morning, a "lurker" named Tush324 emerged with this vote of confidence:

"I wish I could have gone to the Amazon and collected ANY information regarding Survivor. That would have been a thrill of a life time for me.

There have been too many here that put ChillOne to the task and were, at times, too harsh. I no longer frequent this board, that often, because of this type of mentality. You cannot expect someone, who was not there during filming, to know every detail."

Still on that morning of February 21st, hard-core supporter black light poster went after my critics in this post:

"So now the photo of the plaque is doctored?

Wow. Paranoia reigns supreme. You guys missed your calling. A lot of you should have been on Sen. Joe McCarthy's team ferreting out secret members of the communist party in the fifties.

Why is the best explanation for what is here is the one explanation that a whole posse of people are now sure is an outright lie?.......the explanation C1 gives is the most feasible, the most commonsense, and readily accounts for everything he's written. He's a guy who vacationed at the Ariau in January. He's a Survivor fan who got lucky and hooked up with a couple of Brazilians who weren't as circumspect as they should be. Just like you or I would, he pressed these people for a little bit of information. They got part of what they told him right and part of what they told him wrong. Whether due to incomplete memories, incomplete understanding of what was actually happening, translation problems, or maybe even just giving an answer when they didn't even know or pulling his leg now and then, for whatever reason some of it is wrong.

But no, it can't be that easy. The whole thing has to be some grand conspiracy. Interesting phenomenon: People seem to like "finding" big elaborate lies. Like to say "Ha! I was the only one who saw it from the start!" Okay, whatever. IMHO the story's simple and you guys are chasing ghosts…"

I felt grateful for such a deep and reasoned response to my critics at this important moment, but I knew there would be many other voices shouting to be heard. One voice that was a bit troubling to hear belonged to Antithesys, the former thread Administrator, in a post at 12:25 p.m. that day:

"Since the release of the cast list, not ONE piece of intel has come true. Not ONE.

And what's all this talk about Monster Island? I wouldn't have put this in Monster Island. Hoaxes don't go there."

When I read that one, I breathed a sigh of relief that Anti was no longer "in charge" of my thread. I felt even better about the next three posts that rolled in during the next 15 minutes. At 12:26 p.m., jamesriver thanked black light for his post and added, "To me, C1 has gotten too much right and held up for too long under intense skepticism and questioning for the 'simplest explanation' to be that he made up the whole thing."

Then Wezzie, that veteran warrior of the spoiling community and consistent supporter, chimed in: "My personal opinion is that he is what he seems to be…an engineer, a single guy with money, time and desire to travel…. All I can vouch for is the location info, and ChillOne's story meshed with information Dan and I received on September 19 about the camp and TC locations."

Next, JayBerman stepped up and backed off his claim from the night before about how I had concocted my photos:

"My previous posts were speculation on how this *possible* hoax could've been accomplished. However, I could be totally wrong about this individual. He does seem determined and very sincere.

Let's give it some time."

Whew! That was a very positive sign that my strategy was paying off. I got my supporters to speak up with so much conviction and authority that one of my critics was already backing down. As that Friday post-Ep.2 rolled by, I scored another triumph, this one regarding my offer to post more photos from the Ariau. Snewser, whose spoiling reputation is impeccable, offered to take the photos from me and make them available to the board unedited. At the same time, Snewser confirmed that my first round of photos were "not Photoshopped" and had been taken with "an Olympus digital camera."

I immediately agreed to link Snewser to my photo album over the weekend. Dan Bollinger, the other highly respected expert on photos, also came on that afternoon and said, "I'm convinced that all the pictures ChillOne posted are authentic and correctly labeled." With these developments coming from the experts, I was even more confident that the crazy rumors about fabricated photos were about to be squashed for good.

Meanwhile, I eagerly watched as posters new and old voted for keeping my thread alive. Andy4Twins posted:

"I too appreciate ChillOne's post…and I bought into the veracity of the information. I did know the risks and am still interested in seeing how the season play's out. I won't take the information as Gospel, but why the desire to crucify Cool1 is beyond me. If you don't believe any of the information in here is a Spoiler, it is easy enough for you to ignore this thread. There was some Spoiler information that did turn out to be true…leave it here for those of us that enjoy reading it."

Then came a surprise vote from Jedijake, who had been playing both sides until recently becoming more of a skeptic:

"I think it should stay here. While I think there is a lot to this and there is some fishy stuff (whether it be ChillOne or his information) there are some striking coincidences which makes it interesting."

Even when my old nemesis Intelly popped up with an I-told-you-so kind of post later on the 21st, he stopped short of demanding my ouster. The next day, Saturday the 22nd, the votes continued to fall mostly in my column. At 1:26 p.m., an infrequent poster named Golf Man said:

"Hang in there, ChillOne…I've been around for a while which means nothing except for this—I've been through a ton of hoaxes. My ubergut tells me that this is not a hoax."

And five minutes later, another quiet voice, Girlpower101, added:

"I cannot believe you guys are saying that this is not credible!

I still believe that this is credible, only that the source wasn't really aware coz there are approximately 50 staff and crew in survivor, and they wouldn't know who goes first and who goes second, and besides they don't know much about the game."

Yes, the momentum was shifting. My support base was stabilizing and even growing. That was welcome news, but my strategy in handling this precarious period was not complete. I was keeping an eye for an opportunity to quickly rebut any critics as a way to sound the drum beat of support even more loudly and discourage possible new critics from jumping in. At 5:27 p.m., still on the 22nd, I noticed I LUV PENNY post:

"This thread should have been thrown into the crapper once episode 1 aired. ChillOne has been 100% wrong from day 1."

At 5:46 p.m., I shot back:

"You are more than welcome to leave this thread if you think it's a hoax. No one is making you come here.

My question to you is simple…if you're not interested in this thread, why do you keep coming back???

—The ChillOne"

I was taking a more aggressive posture, rather than simply responding to questions posed to me, because I was determined not to be "defeated" by those who like to make a game at spoiling the spoilers. And I was letting the board know of my tougher posture in no uncertain terms. Critics telling me to go away? Well then, I'll just challenge THEM to go away if they didn't want to work this spoiler! At the same time, my supporters sensed I was turning back the tide of naysayers and stepped in to try to help me box them into a corner. In another strong defense at 6:28 p.m. that day, black light poster observed:

"I love all this absolute certainty by the C-1 bashers! It's entertaining. TOTALLY WORTHLESS! TRASH! COMPLETE HOAX! I KNEW IT WAS A ALL A BIG LIE! ZERO VALUE!…HE'S A FRAUD…

Where do we get you people from? How does society produce such absolutists? People unable to distinguish degrees in anything, everything is totally this or else is totally that? People unable or unwilling to acknowledge any correctness in some elements, if there is incorrectness in any other elements.

The many calls for locking this thread after 2 Ep's are wild and laughable."

That was another solid hit from our corner on the verbal front. Meanwhile, I was acting behind the scenes on the photographic evidence front. I had selected 60 more photos from my Amazon trip to send to Snewser. When he posted them for everyone to examine, Orangeena immediately made sure that the entire board took stock of just what they meant about my credibility:

"Thanks, Snews, once again, for taking the time to post ALLLL of those beautiful, revealing pictures. Awesome job, dudes.

EVERYBODY should check them out and THEN say he's still a hoax. Even included are the passport dates, so he was there when he said he was there."

Well, JayBerman obviously checked them out carefully. That was the poster who really came after me about "fabricated" photos right after Ep.2 ended. Although he did admit the next day that maybe that was just speculation on his part, this post at 1:35 a.m. on February 23rd went much further in turning toward my side:

"After careful consideration, I also concur that this is not a hoax in the slightest. The photographic evidence does not lie…

I hereby retract my speculations about how this improbable hoax was perpetrated, and agree that this thread should continue its course, to be eventually placed in Monster Island."

So the photos shut up almost everybody that might have been tempted to paint me as a fake. Of course, some people would never be satisfied. Intelly came on and had the nerve to say the post-production crew plaque was fabricated because the usual *Survivor* mottoes of Outwit, Outplay, and Outlast had been changed to Outdub, Outlog, and Outcut. I didn't think this kind of crazy charge needed any response, especially since the issue was addressed ages ago, but milkshaky did take it on:

"The sign was made in order to give credit to the POST PRODUCTION crew. DUB, CUT, LOG, etc are terms used in editing the show. Duh."

And so, ChillOne had weathered the storm. When Ep.2 ended, people were calling him a fake and demanding his ouster. Now, as we approached Ep.3, the critics were the ones taking the beating. My strategy had been right on the mark. Like a good *Survivor* contestant, I had been totally successful on the OUTWIT side of playing the game. Of course, I got a big helping hand from my supporters. The board was no longer obsessed with my fate. Other juicy topics returned for discussion and debate, including the nudity event that I had predicted with my intel and that had been foreshadowed on *Survivor* during Ep.2. When a question on this topic came to me, I jumped on it:

"Honestly, I'm not sure if I'll ever be 100% certain what my source was referring to with regards to the TJG (Topless Jungle Girl)....*What I'm looking for is some sort of an indication of a "deal" going down. That was the information that was provided to me...that someone gets naked as a direct result of a "deal" made; this deal is also tied in to TC voting. How it plays out...I'm not sure. I'm just reporting what I heard and hoping that the bright minds on this board can help solve this puzzle.*

—The ChillOne"

So I was trying to spark the creative talents of the best spoilers to help solve this nudity mystery. And in this regard, I give the spoiling group an A+. When you looked past the flaming and the BS'ing, you could see that many of these people were doing a great job in marrying the episodes to my intel and helping to fill the gaps in my information. Now that the characters crying for my exit had been debunked, we were all free to go back to work.

Meanwhile, my thread and its reputation continued to grow. Two days before Ep.3, I noticed that well respected veteran spoiler BetOnBlack had tuned in by posting:

"Damn 102 pages! This has to be the biggest spoiler ever."

And the biggest pieces of my spoiler were still ahead: my Final 4, my Final 2 of Matt and Jenna, and my indicator that Jenna was better liked of the two. Most *Survivor* fans could not imagine Jenna winning at this stage of the show because she was being displayed as selfish and spoiled. But Orangeena offered some insightful analysis into how it could happen:

"Listen, I am not a fan of big-tittied barbie girls. Matt is more MY type, so I am in no hurry to crown Jenna the Queen of Survivor: The Amazon, but the thing is ChillOne already did...

But Jenna MAY CHANGE. We see her as unsympathetic, small-minded, petty, self-absorbed, all the stereotypical clichés of a beauty queen. BUT everytime JP (host Jeff Probst) *mentions her, he goes out of his way to say something positive...."*

So as Ep.3, "Girl Power," was about to begin on February 27th, most of us on the board were watching Jenna very closely, both as a fascinating *Survivor* contestant and as a pivotal part of my intel. With Jenna being a swimsuit model, I had to admit that keeping my eyes closely on her was a fun part of my job.

8

RESTORING ORDER

What a difference a week makes! The first posting as Ep.3 played out on CBS on the evening of February 27th proclaimed:

"All I hafta say after tonight's episode is…
Welcome back, ChillOne."

The poster was a lurker named goosE Egg, but others soon picked up on the theme. With Daniel being voted off and Joanna looking even more likely to go in Ep.4, my initial boot order began to more and more resemble what was happening on *Survivor: The Amazon*. Yes, the non-believers would still say I was 0-for-3 because none of my boots came in exactly the correct order, but the wind was definitely shifting in my direction. The flamers were noticeably quiet on my thread all through the night. I'm sure they had been fanning their flames in anticipation of a boot that would have totally thrown my intel out of whack. Their insults certainly would have been even nastier than after Ep.2. But now, with Daniel gone, they would just have to stuff those attacks back into their temp folders. Or better yet, the Recycle Bin.

But at home, I was not gloating at all. I knew that I had executed my most important strategy after Ep.2. Despite the pats on the back for making a "comeback" now, I didn't feel like I had to make any comeback at all. When I sat back and looked at the big picture, I could see in my mind's eye that I was already a winner—and had been from the minute I logged my first message on Survivor-Sucks. I had posted the biggest spoiler of all time more than a month before the season had even begun. Recently, I had been effectively rallying more people to the supporter side of the spoiling fence. My remaining goals now were simple. All I wanted was for my spoiler to become the most memorable, the most accurate, and the most infamous of the spoiling world.

For that to happen, I was hoping for 100% accuracy with my Final 4 of Christy, Butch, Matt, and Jenna. I was studying their characters ever more closely, and like other members of the board I had seen some good signs during

Ep.3. An occasional poster named bluesky made these notes in a 9:33 a.m. posting on February 28th:

*"The 50-year-old guy in the F4…is looking to be Butch (Roger, like Joanna, is
way to abrasive to last)…so who is he allied with? Butch has been almost invisi-
ble…his best scene this week was as the recipient of that fabulous come on from
Jenna…that girl can turn it on big time…the scene had F4, for both of them,
stamped all over it."*

I had to agree with bluesky, and this was an important development. One of
the gaps in my intel was the 50-year-old male: Roger or Butch? I had already
speculated on the board that it was Butch, but the choice wasn't obvious to everyone then. Now, from a *Survivor* editing perspective, Butch was looking real good
for filling those shoes. And, of course, any interaction or potential alliance
between any of my F4 contestants had to be seen as a good thing. So as I observed
Butch and Jenna relating during Ep.3, I was definitely getting more pumped!

I also liked what I was seeing in Jenna's changing character. Not only was she
flirting with Butch, but she was also being noticed by many of the guys in the
male tribe. That was another positive sign for my intel, as noted in a posting by
niknak2010 on March 1st:

*"In the first episode, the men were all agog over Shawna and Heidi. No mention of
Jenna at all. Then they have the "flirting" reward challenge, during which Jenna
works it with her eyes, her tone, her strut, her attitude. Afterwards, suddenly we start
hearing talk about "Jenna's butt" and "Magic 8-Ball, will Jenna notice me?"*

*Strange as it may have sounded a month ago, to a person whose only reference is the
edited-down footage that is shown on Thursday nights, Jenna was not considered very
attractive at first, but is growing on the men as the show progresses. I'm not saying that
in reality nobody thought Jenna was pretty at first, but if someone is just going by
what we've been shown, then CO's description of the F2 girl fits Jenna."*

A few days later, Trixiego posted a similar sentiment:

*"Interesting coincidence in re-watching last week's episode which may have already
been brought up was Roger stating his opinion on Jenna to the effect that she may not
be what he considered a hottie but he isn't dead either.*

*I just found that strikingly familiar to CO's description of what the F2 woman
was described as."*

I considered both of these postings to be very solid observations. Right from
the start of my thread, the spoiling community had placed a great deal of importance on my intel's account that Jenna was "not the most attractive at first" and
vigorously debated what that meant. Initially, this confused everyone. Jenna was
a swimsuit model. How the hell could she not been seen as attractive?

However, it was becoming clearer all the time that my intel had nothing to do with Jenna's looks actually getting better as the show progressed. She had been playing her looks very strategically at first, hiding her "assets" while Heidi and Shawna got all the up-front attention. Now, Jenna was starting to display a little more of her attractiveness to the men. They noticed! So this bit of spoiling information was becoming an important piece in the puzzle.

Christy also continued to look strong enough as a Final 4 contender. I was especially confident in her making it because my source had named "the deaf girl" first when I asked about the Final 4 back at the Ariau. But although I would never say so to the board, I was just a bit concerned about Matt after the first few episodes.

I had no doubt that Matt was the contestant my source was referring to with his description of the F2 male. He was the only one that fit the profile of the big, strong male with a side part in his hair. The problem for me was that Matt looked so big and so strong that he stood out for his physical prowess among the male contestants. By *Survivor* tradition, strong men tend to stick around early on because they are regarded as assets in the challenges. Over the long haul, however, they are seen as threats and are targeted to be voted off starting around the middle episodes of the season. Fortunately for me, Matt appeared to recognize this possibility. He was putting a lot of effort into doing chores for the male tribe, and during Ep.3 he had befriended Daniel after Daniel's run-in with Roger. So Matt was demonstrating solid strategy. He'd need a lot more of that to stay out of trouble over the next several weeks, and I just hoped he had it in him. I had a lot banking on him.

For the moment, though, there wasn't much for me to do. I purposely decided not to post for awhile after Ep.2. With this absence, I was toying with the board just a bit. I wanted to portray my confidence through my silence, and I also wanted to see how long it took for someone to notice that I hadn't been posting. An infrequent poster named rockmyworld noticed and made this posting on the morning of March 3rd:

"Looks like the last post by ChillOne was on 2/25.

I look forward to, and miss his comments.

I suppose ChillOne and BlackLightPoster are keeping their conversations private, no doubt tired of the bashing received here.

Please come back ChillOne and BlackLightPoster!"

I smiled when I saw this invitation and immediately responded:

"Can't speak for BLP, but I've been here all along…haven't gone anywhere. Did not feel like I could contribute anything interesting lately, so I've just been reading and hanging about. And, about the bashing…no worries. I've learned to deal with it.

You know, one of the things I mentioned way back in January (one of my spoilers) was that the men lose many of the challenges up front; causing great tension. Looks like that one has certainly come true. Sticking with my intel (even being a bit off with boot order) looking for Joanna to exit this week. After that, looking for my Final 4 spoiler to materialize.

Enjoy.

—The ChillOne"

With this posting, the board could clearly see me in a confident light. As far as those rumors about my interacting with black light poster behind the scenes, they were, like most rumors about me, totally false. It was natural, I suppose, to wonder if BLP and I were strategizing because BLP was such a big supporter of me and my intel. But the truth was that BLP and I never corresponded off-line. In fact, throughout the entire thread I never strategized with anyone off-line as far as what and how to post. I also never appeared as "multiple" people, using a second or third posting alias to pump up a point I had been trying to make or to strengthen ChillOne's profile. Rumors, rumors, and more rumors. After awhile, I realized they just came with the territory.

But the rumor mill was quiet as we all turned our attention to Ep.4 on March 6th. And when Joanna got the boot, my intel was looking more solid than at any point since just before the first episode. CCBIGGs55 was the first to call it at 9:58 p.m. that evening:

"3/4 ChillOne…Way to Go

You know you have to be on to something…real.

You are quoted all over the spoiler boards…

Only got to watch last 20 min and thought it looked like Shawna (as the one who would be voted off)*…but knew that C1 said Joanna…*

You rock. You are the spoiler KING!"

Well, the critics weren't going to let the 3/4 scorecard pass without a different interpretation. Antithesys immediately shot back:

"Interesting counting basis you have, because I count 0/4. Are you using the metric system?"

I decided to enter the fray just a few minutes later that evening with this post:

"Well, I'll admit it. Technically, Anti is correct (from a boot order perspective)…on the other hand. From a contestant perspective, 3/4 is not too shabby. One might even goes so far as to argue that my source was 4/4; however, this could never be

proved right or wrong since nobody can say who my source was truly thinking about when he described the 30-ish y/o lady.

Anti…I'll "go out on a limb" and say I'll make up my 0/4 showing to you by going 4/4 in the final 4…

Stay tuned.

—The ChillOne"

That posting made it look like I was cocky about the Final 4. Well, I was confident. And I certainly was feeling good that order had been restored to the board as my intel boot picks had fallen more into line. My critics and flamers had mostly fallen silent. Maybe some of them realized that I really was telling the truth, or maybe they were simply re-strategizing. But even without their pestering, I wasn't really all that cocky. I actually had a different motive with this posting. It was more strategy on my part. I was playing the spoiling game. I'll explain how.

With the passing of Ep.4, and with no new intel about boot order until the Final 4, I knew we were about to enter a down period on the thread. So I was trying to build up more excitement to keep the thread lively. As CCBIGGs55 noted in their posting at the conclusion of Ep.4, the other spoiling forums were talking up my spoiler. ChillOne appeared to have some thread running on almost every spoiling board, both public and private. While visiting some of these other forums, I spotted several direct copies of my original posts from Sucks. Some sites even had direct links to my thread at Sucks. And comments such as, "Oh, you're on the ChillOne bandwagon" or "That doesn't match with what C1 says" served as evidence that the debate over my intel extended far and wide. Of course, since I was the only major spoiler out there for the S6 season, it had to be debated.

So ChillOne's reputation was certainly growing. But I still wanted my SurvivorSucks thread to remain THE hot spot. I wanted to be the biggest ever. So I made that bold prediction about going 4/4 in the Final 4 to keep things rocking. It didn't take much of a push for my main supporters to respond by talking up my Final 4. The first was black light poster:

"Congratulations C1. 3 out of 4 of the first four booted people even if not the correct order. Plus the site info, the deaf girl spoiler, topless jungle girl…who I think is still to come. Great work.

…The odds against picking 3 of the first 4 as a group I could calculate if I wanted to bother, but I won't; rest assured they're long, long odds. If any of the critics and naysayers made similar calls themselves a month before air time, somehow I missed it…

So now that the first block is history, I've seen enough that I'll go ahead and stick my neck out and say I'm betting your F4 proves correct."

Orangeena was still insisting that I was 4/4 in naming the people voted off in the first four boots. To make her case, she kept arguing that Janet actually could fit the description of my source's reference to a woman about 30:

"...to an impoverished river boatman, Janet could look 30-ish. I mean, have you ever seen a Brazilian native woman in that age bracket? Life is hard there and by Janet's real age, a peasant woman would there look MUCH older, compared to Jane...

I have no doubt that your F4 is correct."

In my response to the board on whether Janet possibly could be my source's 30-year-old female, I admitted, "I do not feel she fits this description, but, in the eyes of my source...maybe she did. We'll never know." Anyway, whether 3/4 or 4/4, my source had come through better than what most people were expecting when *Survivor: The Amazon* began. Newcomers continued to praise my intel, and before the night of Ep.4 was over, Wezzie hailed me as "The King of Spoilers for S-Amazon!"

So my support base was solid, and with my bold prediction of going 4/4 in my Final 4 I knew the debates about my spoiler would continue. But that by itself would not be enough to keep this thread lively for the next seven or eight episodes. I believed that the spoilers of this spoiling room needed to get back to serious spoiling again. So on the morning after Ep.4, I picked up on a comment from one poster who said that everyone was on their own now until the Final 4:

"Possibly, but, you do have F4 information. You can work backwards. You can use my F4 information to formulate alliances, boot order, etc. IMHO (in my humble opinion), it makes these upcoming 'middle episodes' of S6 interesting and fun to watch."

With this invitation, I was trying to get people to realize that even though I did not have any specific details about the middle episodes, there was plenty of spoiling to be done. What was the boot order going to be leading up to the F4? What other clues might be obtained that might point to Matt more clearly as the F2 male, for those who didn't trust my interpretation of what my source meant? For example, how much weight did he lose over the course of the season? Studying weight loss had been used as a predictor in the spoiling community for years. Also, how could some of the other popular contestants fall before the F4? What mistakes in strategy would do them in?

I knew that the people posting on Sucks were a very determined group of spoilers and that they would eventually get back on track to spoiling activity. Because this was really the first time that they had been handed so much information on a silver platter so early in the season, I suspect that many of them did not know what to do when this lull in my spoiler arrived. They had been so used to working with my intel that they forgot how to spoil the old-fashioned way—by sifting through snippets from the episodes or the previews looking for clues, studying possible alliances, etc. So, much like my source's intel that the Topless Jungle Girl had to be "kick-started" to get more involved in the *Survivor* game, I concluded that these spoilers had to be "kick-started" to get more involved in our game again.

As I turned them loose, I got out of the way. I simply clarified my interpretation of my source's Final 4 again by naming Jenna, Matt, Butch, and Christy as the last four survivors, and then I refrained from speculating how that Final 4 would get through the upcoming middle episodes. I had learned my lesson about mixing in too much of my own speculation with my intel. I was a much more experienced agent now. Like the successful *Survivor* contestants, I would stand back and let others make the mistakes. If I were to get tripped up along the way, it would not be because of something foolish I had done. It would only happen if my source, the now famous Uncle Boat Driver, had remembered wrong or gotten mixed up while revealing to me the biggest secrets of *Survivor*.

I had wanted to be the one to expose those secrets. And now I was getting so close to my goal I could smell it as strong as the smoke from a fire in the Amazon.

9

JUNGLE FEVER

As *Survivor: The Amazon* rolled into the middle episodes, we were all caught up in the drama and intrigue of the show. S6 was attracting big audiences for CBS, with fans everywhere becoming more invested in the fate of characters like Christy, a sentimental favorite for many as the first-ever deaf survivor, and other popular contestants. Meanwhile, over on SurvivorSucks, our lively band of spoilers was more and more gripped by the suspense over whether ChillOne's Final 4 would make it through to the season finale—and if so, how?

The case for my F4 intel grew stronger with each passing week. Here's how it looked from my seat:

Ep.5, "Pick-Up Sticks," March 13: With Jeanne being voted off, my source looked even more on target with his memory of the early boots. Jeanne certainly could fit the mold of that 30-year-old female he had tagged as one of the first four boots. So one could easily argue that Uncle Boat Driver had correctly named four of the first five to go. For some, an air of inevitably about my F4 coming true was already settling in. One theory suggested that Mark Burnett and the other folks at SEG would be so angry at seeing the season spoiled that they'd file a lawsuit against those responsible for my leak. And one pesky poster named sunsawed announced during the night of Ep.5:

"Congratulations to ChillOne for RUINING Survivor 6!...

Now nobody has any reason to think about Survivor again! All you have to do is look at the boards and ChillOne will provide you with your answer.

'If you don't wanna know don't go'!

And I shant."

Well, sunsawed really wasn't going anywhere, as it soon became clear, and neither were most of the others on the board. At this point I understood quite well that spoilers are spoilers. They can't help keep coming back. After all, spoiling is an addiction of sorts. If they weren't caught up in the fever of spoiling the outcome, why would they come to a forum clearly marked with full warnings that spoiling is the aim?

Anyway, as I would argue many times, spoiling is not ruining. To ruin a show is to force people to read and review information of what was going to occur in some forum or environment populated by those who clearly do not want to know. It's tipping them off to something they didn't ask for. Spoiling, on the other hand, is telling people what's going to happen, based on whatever clues you believe you have deciphered, in a place where everyone DOES want to know the result and welcomes it. It is done in a forum that warns that the information posted there should only be reviewed, monitored, and discussed by individuals interested in having the secrets of the show revealed before they are aired.

Still, with spoilers being prone to contrariness, this "ruining" label had its backers. Later that evening, SamCahill compared spoiling with opening Christmas presents days before the holiday, taking away the surprise. I could acknowledge that this might be true for *Survivor* fans outside of the spoiling community. The majority of them probably would not want to know the outcome of the season before the finale. Even when I watched S1-S5, I didn't want to know who won ahead of time. But once you become a spoiler, your outlook shifts completely. Then you're caught up in the entertainment of seeing whether the spoiler will come true.

I just shrugged off these comments about ruining the show as another sign of the magnitude of what was happening. It was a completely new experience out there in spoiler land. Could an ENTIRE season truly be spoiled? At the same time, I also still felt concerned that these remarks could discourage some people from sticking with the board. That, I couldn't shrug off. So in my own post on the morning after Ep.5, I said:

"PLEASE do not assume that my F4 includes Butch and Matthew. This is my speculation based on my intel. There are others that fit these descriptions....

PEOPLE...there is a lot of game to be played here. Can anyone predict what's going to happen between now and the F4??? We may get some spoilers, but the entire show is NOT spoiled. There are MANY weeks before the F4. A lot can happen. There is NO guarantee that my source is 100% accurate on the F4 (however, I personally think he is)."

No, I was not suffering any loss of confidence about fingering Butch and Matt for the Final 4. While I couldn't be sure my intel was right because it didn't come from inside CBS, I still believed in it. I was simply employing another tactic here. If I gave the spoilers room to doubt, they'd keep debating. The thread would stay hot, which was always good news for me. I was having far too much fun reading all the fascinating and crazy posts to have it even slow down.

And I still had the critics to joust with. After sunsawed's apparently sarcastic remarks about leaving the board, she shot a fiery flame in the wee early morning hours of March 15th. When I got up and saw it that morning, I immediately sat down for a little return volley. I set up my usual practice of opening two screens, one for scanning sunsawed's post and selecting excerpts, the other to type my responses. I began my post by observing, "Wow, awfully cranky huh. Have a bad day???" Then I plucked through some of sunsawed's points and shot back my answers. (My comments appear in boldface after sunsawed's remarks in italics):

"I believe 100% that you went to Brazil for the SOLE PURPOSE of spoiling Survivor...."

"OK...hmmmm, tell me how you know this??? Let me remind the forum (and you) that my sole purpose of going to Brazil was to party with a group of friends of mine in Rio de Janeiro for New Years. I spent about 80% of my time there. Made a side trip to Iguacu Falls and the Ariau...If you'd like, I could post 200 of my photos just from New Years Eve in Rio."

"The kicker is where you post that Jana is more liked that F2 guy. How the hell would some, non-English speaking flunky know that???"

"Now you are an expert on Brazilian mentality. Wow, I'm totally blown away. How do people know the things they know???"

"Obviously you have some ENGLISH speaking source (from CBS) which, for obvious reasons, you need to protect."

"Hmmmm...sorry to disappoint you, ummmmm, but, I really don't."

"So obviously, you are King of Spoilers forever and ever Amen. My only request is for you to SAVE YOUR SOUL and CONFESS."

"I did not give myself this title...And now you're getting all Joanna, Amen, biblical on me....OK, so I'll confess. I am sorry for posting information on this site. I am sorry that I have found out some things about the show and decided to use this forum as a means of communication. Man, I'm so sorry folks..."

Notice that I didn't use one cap in my responses to sunsawed, a signal that I wasn't angry at all. I was actually laughing as I replied. And I knew I got the desired response from the board when Jedijake posted:

"ChillOne's defense of his claims is the only thing keeping this thread alive. It's the reason many people (including myself) keep coming back....If Chill didn't defend himself, this thread would be dead. We WANT the discussion."

As Ep.6 dawned, the only downer for me was realizing that I almost definitely would not hear back from Enrique after my follow-up attempt to establish email contact with him in hopes of shedding further light on my source's Final 4. I wondered: Did SEG really re-visit the Ariau? Was Enrique in trouble? Was he scolded and ordered not to communicate with me? Did Enrique lose his job? Did my source, the now famous Uncle Boat Driver, lose his job? Though I realized there was nothing I could do about it, I remained concerned—and I still am today.

Ep.6, "More Than Meets the Eye," March 19: Shawna got the boot. In another significant development, my intel's reference to a nudity scene was previewed, with Heidi and Jenna apparently stripping down in the next episode. While the board debated whether this was a proper thing for a schoolteacher like Heidi to do and speculated on how the parents and school administrators would respond, I just chalked up the nudity preview as another "hit" from my source. More important than this specific spoiler panning out, every member of my Final 4 was still holding on. And the countdown was continuing.

On the board, the spoilers were studying my Final 4 as closely as I was. Not only were they looking for alliances that would make my F4 possible, but they were also noticing how Mark Burnett was editing these four contestants. Orangeena, always a top investigator, addressed this in a post on March 22nd:

"Knowing that ChillOne has let us in on knowing that Matt and Jenna are the likely F2, it is fascinating to me to watch how EPMB develops their "characters" in the editing.

I think they are both getting positive editing. Esp. when you compare the way Jenna is portrayed to the way Heidi is portrayed. I guess Heidi is the S6 villain…

Matt's editing is very complex.

Correct me if I'm wrong, but he does seem to be getting a lot of crocodile imagery. Crocs—Lying low in the water, watching everything, then devouring all the birds (Jabaru) and the fish (Tambaqui).

Also, when Rob was talking about Matt being good at catching fish, so therefore he'd stick around for another Tribal Council or two (always famous Survivor last words), the camera cut to Matt, then panned to the Lonnnnnnnnng string of fish that Matt had caught that were being nicely cooked over the roaring fire.

ChillOne's F2 sounded improbable at first and also for the first few Ep's too many, but NOW LOOK WHAT'S HAPPENED. Matt and Jenna ARE ON THE SAME TEAM AND HAVE ALLIED.

CHILLONE RULES. And it's actually exciting to see how his spoilers keep coming true one by one…"

During that episode, I noted the reshuffling of the two tribes and reasoned that this was what my source meant by his reference to a merging of tribes fairly early in S6. The two tribes had not been combined into one, but some previously separated members merged together in the crossover. Matt, for one, admitted he was relieved at the switch because he had felt "like my head was on the chopping block at Tambaqui." As it was, he still was fingered as one of the two possible contestants to be voted off, until Rob observed, "I finally get Matt eating out of the palm of my hand, and they want me to vote him off." So Matt was spared, and Shawna's torch was extinguished. Rob was emerging as an extremely crafty player, and I found myself appreciating his moves more in every episode. And just maybe, I was playing our "game" on the board almost as well as Rob.

In the mean time, while I logged regular long hours on SurvivorSucks I still kept busy in the rest of my life. I had begun to share the story of my spoiling adventure and my SurvivorSucks notoriety with a few other people, especially my brother, my buddy Puddin' Head, and my Dad. Neither of my parents were extremely Internet-savvy, but my Dad was net-literate enough to start tuning in. And in the weeks between Ep.6 and Ep.7, I had begun to tune into another major competition. My alma mater, Syracuse, was beginning its participation in the NCAA basketball tournament. The first two games were in Boston, but getting the time off or the tickets proved too difficult for me. Watching on CBS at home, I thoroughly enjoyed their victories in the first two rounds, moving them into the Sweet Sixteen.

Ep.7, "Girls Gone Wilder," March 26: Wow! The nude scene did happen, and it did involve a deal of sorts as Heidi and Jenna bared not only their breasts but their "everything" in exchange for peanut butter and chocolate. I certainly had my eyes open to a scene that James Bond himself would certainly appreciate, but my gaze mostly remained fixated on the Tribal Council vote and the fate of my Final 4. And with Roger voted out in this episode, my conclusion that Butch was the 50-year-old male that my source had identified as part of the Final 4 was now solidified.

At the same time, Matt was being depicted as a bit of a wacko with his aggressive behavior. I recognized this for what it was: a red herring. Matt was trying to convince the other players he wasn't a threat in terms of playing the game, and CBS was editing him to be an unlikely F2 or even F4 finisher. These were all positive signs for me and my intel.

Meanwhile, Jenna continued to impress the board as a more likely F2 bet…and possible winner of S6. OzarkSurvivor posted this analysis a few hours after the end of Ep.7:

"After seeing tonight's episode, I am convinced that Jenna wins…Deena is too sure of herself, whereas Jenna, while some of y'all may hate her, is generally keeping everything real and easygoing.

For instance, at Jabaru's first TC, when Jenna responds to Christy's comment about no one doing work:

'I think it's kind of insulting to say that we just sit around.'

(this shows that she doesn't think it's fair to point fingers at your own teammates)

Then, tonight's TC, about jumping off so quickly:

'Hey, if either Heidi or myself get voted off tonight because we wanted peanut butter and chocolate cookies, it was totally worth it because we had fun.'

(shows that she's still able to have fun, even with the game in play)

Also, when she commented on Heidi going to Tambaqui:

'She is just my rock here and I don't know what I'm going to do without her.'

That comment set up Jenna's personal struggle: Dependency on others. She's now able to take the game without her rock, Heidi, and do it on her own.."

Later that evening, Orangeena keyed in on Jenna's continued changes in her physical appearance:

"…is it my imagination or is Jenna really starting to look REALLY pretty—in the face, I mean? Her close-ups are VERY flattering. She IS becoming the most beautiful (or hottest) woman on the tribe!

So C1 is still with us. And I do think it's Matt and Jenna."

Off the board, the spoiling community gained even more notoriety when *The New York Times* ran an article about the popularity of spoiler websites. The article revealed that the folks at CBS do keep a watchful eye on what happens there and that Mark Burnett thought that the spoilers' interest was good for the show. The article did not mention ChillOne at all, but there was a reason for that. I actually was approached by the newspaper to be interviewed, but I told them I would agree only if they referred to me exclusively by my alias, ChillOne. They said they could only use me as a source if they used my real name, so I declined the interview.

When the story came out, I saw that Dan Bollinger was featured in it. So were Tom Gilman, a.k.a. Snewser, who runs SurvivorNews.net, and Jeff Pittman from TrueDorkTimes. But as important as the exposure might have been for me, it was not a tough choice for me to say no and I had no second thoughts about it. Had I used my real name, I would have been deluged with personal emails, some of them the threatening type. I really didn't know just whom I was interacting with out there, so it felt safer to maintain the anonymity. Then again, the mystery regarding ChillOne, and who he really was, also was worth preserving. But even without SurvivorSucks or my spoiler being mentioned, our board was impressed by all the attention given to spoiling. Orangeena posted:

"I think it's GRRRRREAT that the NYTimes, the paper of record, has now admitted that WE ALL HERE in spoilerland and Tim (Snews) and Jeff (TDT) are now all a force to be reckoned with in television…

I think it's significant in that whether ChillOne is right or not (and I think he more or less is) that the boards ARE read by CBS, EPMB and obviously REPORTERS AT THE NYTIMES!?! Who knew?"

Of course, just because the spoiling community suddenly became more famous across the nation didn't mean that the conversations on forums like SurvivorSucks always sounded upright and sophisticated. Hey, this was still an Internet forum. Some posters just had a certain tendency to act in absurd ways, and going "mainstream" wasn't about to make them clean up their act. Intelly started another trail of accusations about the earlier newspaper column in the *Orange County Register* in California, saying he couldn't understand why if I lived in the East I was contacting a newspaper in the West. Well, I didn't contact that reporter. The reporter contacted me to request an interview. This time, I let my supporters respond, and the exchanges between milkshaky and Intelly were entertaining, if not ready for prime-time national exposure. At one point Intelly was chiding milkshaky for responding to one of his nasty posts that he was trying to get me to answer:

"Is it time to take another picture of someone in a baggy clown suit Milky? That is your claim to fame is it not. Verbal battles are not your strong suit you have to short of a wick. You try to get personnel in your attacks like a little school boy, NANANANA you spelled that wrong. Wow, its time to start acting your age. Only what you question has merit is a little self centered even for you. Are you trying out for the part of a guard dog or just that lonely willing to start a fight just to have someone to talk to?"

Half an hour later, milkshaky shot back:

"If your questions attained an ounce of intelligence or even common sense, I wouldn't be jumping all over you. What does it MATTER if he responded to a reporter who HAPPENS to live somewhere in the Western United States?…

Your inane questions and pathetic attempts to sound like an English Scholar is what makes you the clown with the baggy suit."

I just sat back and took it all in, accepting the silliness as part of the fare on an open-forum Internet group. I also kept my sense of humor during another bizarre moment that week between Ep.7 and Ep.8 of *Survivor: The Amazon*. Suddenly, everything I had posted on the board just disappeared! Gone without a trace or an explanation. While the board went crazy trying to figure out why this had happened and what it meant for my spoiler, the obvious answer didn't sink in right away. It was simply a great April Fool's Day joke.

Anyway, I was generally in good spirits the weekend between those two Thursday night episodes for another reason. Syracuse had knocked off Auburn and Oklahoma to make it to the NCAA basketball tournament's Final Four! As a diligent agent, I didn't put much stock in omens, but I sure didn't mind having my alma mater's basketball team alive in the Final Four while my intel of *Survivor*'s Final 4 also was alive and kickin'!

Ep.8, "Sleeping with the Enemy," April 3: And the road to the Final 4 for Christy, Butch, Matt, and Jenna continued, with Dave getting voted off this time. The first post of the night asked how anyone could still doubt ChillOne's spoiler and took it as a foregone conclusion that Matt and Jenna would make the Final 2, with Jenna 95% likely to win it all.

So the board, in its continued response to my spoiler, was zeroing in on a Matt-Jenna F2. Apparently, so were some gamblers in those on-line casinos that take wagers on *Survivor*. They were putting big money on a Matt-Jenna show-down. At least one, and possibly more venues apparently shut down all betting action on *Survivor: The Amazon* because they reportedly traced a couple of these big Matt-Jenna wagers back to CBS employees who also had bet on past *Survivor* finalists correctly. When this news hit the spoiling community, it lent more credibility to my spoiler and a Matt-Jenna F2. An article on PopPolitics.com written by Chris Wright also jumped in and thoroughly analyzed the rise of my spoiler since I first began my thread.

For fans of *Survivor* who only paid attention to the spoiling boards, it might have appeared that almost everyone in America was expecting a Matt-Jenna finale. Not! As it turned out, a CBS poll of *Survivor* fans about this time suppos-edly revealed that Matt and Jenna were considered the LEAST likely of the remaining contestants to win it all. I wondered why. Perhaps it had a lot to do with how well Rob was playing the game. Or maybe it was because Christy was still the sentimental favorite. Or maybe it was reflective of the negative editing spin that MB kept putting on Matt (a psycho) and Jenna (a bitch) to combat the ChillOne spoiler. The vast majority of the fans voting were most likely not attuned to the spoiling community and the conversations we all had been wrapped up in for almost three months. They were in another world.

As for me, I was still tuning in to my thread practically every waking minute that I wasn't working or at the gym. Except, that is, for two "blackout" peri-ods—one on Saturday evening, April 5, and then again on Monday night, April 7. On those nights I shut off my thread and was glued to CBS for a different kind of show. Syracuse defeated Texas and then Kansas to win the National Championship! I watched it all at home, then later rushed out to get the *Sports Illustrated* with Syracuse star Carmello Anthony on the cover and hung it in my office. I thought about posting a little mention of this on the thread but held back, at least for awhile. The other "big game" was still very much undecided.

Ep.9, "The Chain," April 10: Deena got booted. Whew! My Final 4 was safe for another week. Actually, it would be another two weeks because the April 17 episode would be devoted to reviewing what had happened in *Survivor: The Amazon* up to that point. The next new episode was set for April 24th.

The alliances between the remaining players were murky as to how they could result in my F4 making it, but I wasn't worried. I trusted my source. I felt relaxed, and I even dropped in a reference to my being a "proud Syracuse grad" a week or so after the championship.

I also enjoyed Orangeena's April 19th reference to my story being "MORE INTERESTING than the show as its played out." Well, I wanted to believe that my thread was at least AS interesting as the real *Survivor* on TV. My thread had it all: a lively and colorful cast of characters, interesting twists and turns, controversy, suspense, humor. It was intellectually stimulating, at least at times. We had good guys and bad guys. We had our own people voted off. We had spoilers spoiling the spoiler. As I often observed, we had become true reality TV in the form of this Internet message thread.

Things were starting to look almost too good on the board, especially when Intelly stepped up and, out of the blue, made this proclamation the day before Ep.10:

"OK I GIVE UP! CHILLONE = SPOILER GOD
My whole world is turned upside-down"

I had no idea what had prompted Intelly's change of heart. Maybe his entire mission had been to try to break me and spoil my spoiler. Since it had not worked, Intelly was throwing in the towel and shaking my hand. Whatever triggered this public about-face, I accepted the gesture.

Ep.10, "Q & A," April 24: First post after the show belonged to a lurker named kittycollector:

"ChillOne! YOU RULE!
Alex is gone.
This thread has become part of the game. Will it play out as predicted? Every week the answer gets closer to YES."

I watched the episode on the edge of my seat. I knew as Ep.10 began that each of the remaining episodes would be totally nerve-racking for all of us, especially me. On the board, I would still appear calm, cool, and collected. I still had to be the suave secret agent. But at home I was totally animated, especially with the developments of Ep.10, a major turning-point episode.

That night, Rob had decided to switch alliances and join Matt, Christy, and Butch. So they decided to pick off Alex. This really ticked off Heidi and Jenna because Rob had betrayed them. If Rob had stayed with the Alex-Jenna-Heidi alliance, Matt would have been voted off in Ep.10 and my F2 would have been shot. Now, my F4 was really shaping up. Here's how I saw it going the rest of the way:

Matt, Butch, and Christy were properly aligned, but how would Jenna get there? She and Heidi were outnumbered 4-2. She had to go on some sort of an immunity challenge run, which would have to begin in Ep.11 on May 1st. On that night, Heidi would be voted off, which would fulfill a separate spoiler put out by milkshaky early on. Then, in the following episode, Jenna would win immunity again and Rob would be voted off. That would bring my Final 4 home free!

Yes, everything pointed to this outcome. Matt was coming out of his shell, showing how he had successfully "played" everyone with his wacko act and had been learning strategy tricks from Rob. Now he was positioned to out-maneuver Rob into the F4.

As I read Orangeena politely call me "the greatest guy who ever posted here," I began to think back to the life span of my thread. I had done my best to diligently answer all the many questions posed to me and to treat people with the respect owed them. I tried to play the game, to Outwit and Outplay my challengers on the board. Now, all that was left was for me to Outlast them to the finish line with my 100% accurate F4 and my correct F2 of Matt and Jenna. Nothing was going to stop me now.

Or so it seemed….

10

FLAMES IN THE NIGHT

Long before Ep.11 came to its shocking conclusion, I could see that Christy was in trouble. And if Christy was in trouble, ChillOne was in trouble. Deep, deep trouble. Fiery hot insults trouble.

Christy, the first deaf contestant in *Survivor* history, was my source's first reference when I asked him who reached the Final 4 of *Survivor: The Amazon*. Uncle Boat Driver clearly had said "the deaf girl" was in. And throughout the life of my thread, Christy had been the only absolute, no-speculation, no-need-for-interpretation lock of my intel's F4. The 50-year-old man, at first, could have been either Roger or Butch. The big, strong 26-year-old guy conceivably could have fit at least three of the eight male contestants, although I was clear in my own mind that it had to be Matt. Even Uncle Boat Driver's Jana/Jenna could have been Shawna, if you bought into the Portuguese pronunciation debate. But Christy? Her pick was as clear as glass. And in the ChillOne thread, Christy was the biggest test of whether my F4 would hold up.

And there she was waffling when the alliances were coming unglued and the Tribal Council vote was up in the air. Heidi and Jenna tried to get her to join them to vote off one of the guys. No deal. Rob tried to get her to join him, and most likely Matt, to vote off Heidi. No thanks, she would keep her plans secret. Plans? Christy was simply displaying dumb strategy. And I was worried.

According to the scenario that would fit my intel, and an independent spoiler about Heidi's boot placement, Heidi was supposed to get the boot that night. As the show progressed, I thought there was still a chance that this would happen, especially when Jenna won the Immunity Challenge. But then Jenna made a startling move on a night full of surprises. She gave the Immunity necklace to Heidi!

"Wait a minute," I said to myself. "That's not supposed to happen. Heidi is supposed to go. Now what?"

And I watched fearfully as Rob approached Heidi and Jenna to vote off Christy, even though they were still furious at him for backstabbing them and their alliance in the last Tribal Council vote. But somehow they agreed, and in a 4-2 vote Christy was gone. And one gaping hole had just been blown on my F4 spoiler boat.

I knew what this meant for my thread. A bloody piece of steak had just been dropped into an Amazon River, and the piranhas were about to come swarming. I was the filet, and it was feeding time.

"liar, liar, pants on fire."

"Seems there's some splainin' to do…"

"Lamest hoax ever. Someone seriously should have their throat torn out."

"This spoiler should stay up here as a testament to MB's powers of manipulation. You got bamboozled, led a-stray…duped. SUCKAS."

"I'll bet C1 is really upset with him (Mark Burnett) *for running the Ep's out of order…"*

Those were just some of the early posts. When Jedijake came on for his turn in the blood bath, it was still only 9:52 p.m., with the flames already shooting high into the night sky:

"No affiliation with CBS, huh ChillOne? I've been diplomatic with my skepticism, but now I can say with a smile on my face 'GO TO HELL YOU WORTHLESS SCUM!' There-done."

The attack crew must have been frothing at their keyboards when Ep.11 began, and now they were spewing out their poison so fast and furious that the message board almost crashed. I had wanted to post right away. Do some damage control. Assure people yet again that I was not a hoaxer. Appeal to their sense of reason that my spoiler should not be judged 100% on my boot order, with all the other accurate information I had provided. Remind them that if Butch, Matt, and Jenna made it past next week's Tribal Council vote, I would have 3 of my F4 still intact. Make it clear that I was not running away, despite this stunning setback.

I knew that such a message would be the best strategy. Only problem was, for more than an hour I couldn't get on to post it! I kept getting the message: PAGE CANNOT BE DISPLAYED. When I finally got through at 9:56 p.m., I didn't even know what Jedijake had just posted. I didn't try to respond to any specific questions or criticism, as I usually would. I just wanted to get something out there before too much damage had been done:

"Well, my source was wrong. A lot of you will add the word "AGAIN" to that, but that's fine. A lot of you will say that I'm BS and a liar…kinda harsh in my book, but I'm cool with that too; however, before posting, I challenge you to preface your flames with your contributions this season. You know, there were plenty of correct spoilers

that I've posted this season…way back in January. I also provided pictures. Don't I deserve some credit for them??? Just a hypothetical question.

I will continue to stand by my post.

—*The ChillOne"*

In front of my computer screen, what I was REALLY feeling was a crushing sadness. I felt as if I had let the entire spoiling world down. I had wanted most of all for my F4 to prove 100% accurate, not so much to shut up all the flamers and non-believers but rather to fulfill my mission. Once I had that opportunity to gather intel on *Survivor* in the Amazon, once I had my opening to assume the role of an undercover spy, I wanted to bring the information about this critical part of the series safely home, deliver it, and see it through to its completion. Now I knew that it would be something at least a little less than 100%. Yes, it still could prove to be the biggest spoiler ever if a Matt-Jenna final emerged, but this was a stiff blow to the chin.

"…you can still go to hell…you are evil."

That was Jedijake's next flame. But he wasn't even the nastiest critic of the long, long night that rolled into the next morning. SamCahill began his post with "All I have to say is fuck you ChillOne, fuck you." But the distinction of nastiest poster went to mediadeeva. One of her tamer posts said:

"The boys at CBS and MB are probably pissing their pants over this."

With the flames shooting all around me, I tried to keep my focus. Looking ahead to the next episode, I knew that as long as either Heidi or Rob was voted off in Ep.12, I'd have 75% of my F4 correct. I would certainly take that, but it would be better for Rob to be voted off in that episode and for Heidi to sneak into the F4. That way, I could have sort of an "out" that my source confused Heidi and Christy in his F4 lineup. In any case, I still had Matt and Jenna. And more important, they were properly aligned.

I kept watching the posts rapidly rolling in on the thread. Bing! Bing! Bing! This had to have been the most shocking boot of all *Survivor* history, the shot heard round the spoiling world! Some of the lowlights included:

- During the initial wave of flaming, I could actually imagine some of these people drooling as they posted. At times, it could even seem funny.

- Some of the flames took the form of new demands for the thread to be locked.

- Sprinkled in among the attacks were the posts from a few theorists trying to open up debates about how my boot order might be correct, but just shifted to the left. In other words, what my source reported as the F4 actually referred to the last four people off before the F2 was revealed. So, in this scenario, Christy would be followed off by Butch, Matt, and Jenna, leaving a Final 2 of Rob and Heidi. An interesting twist.

- More claims that I had to be a hoax or part of a CBS plot.

- People actually associated with *Survivor* were probably laughing at all of us Sucksters.

- Almost two and a half hours into the carnage, Anti chimed in with his thanks to ChillOne and defended him a bit. He also coined the label Uncle ChillOne, which did not get used at all by other posters.

- Christy's boot also meant that milkshaky had been proven wrong in his intel that Heidi would be booted off in this episode. At least I had some company.

- Seraphaem posted!!! One of the legends of spoiling came out of the woodwork to put in his two cents.

- Jessiethebrat created a scorecard of ChillOne intel, showing many "wrongs."

- Some posters concluded that the CBS betting scandal involving a Matt-Jenna final also had to be a hoax.

At least people were speaking from their hearts. Well, at least most of them were. Some were speaking from…somewhere else. And some of my supporters managed to squeeze onto the thread here and there. Sam Buru said:

"…if anything C1 made this week's show the best one ever! Thanks Chill, the F2 is still out there! ChillOne, we love ya baby!"

A few lurkers poked their heads up to tell me I was still okay in their books. My Dad also called me on the phone. By now, he was much more aware of the strategy on *Survivor* and the impact of this night's twist on my thread. "What are you going to do now?" he wanted to know, and he told me to hang in there.

I wanted to post again, but even as the night grew late it was still difficult to get through. So I shut my computer down and headed off toward bed. No point in watching more flames anyway. I was mentally exhausted from replaying all the developments of Ep.11, still trying to figure out how it all happened. And now Butch looked like he was hanging out there by himself, vulnerable to being voted off next week. That would leave only Matt and Jenna in the F4, a mere 50% of intel accuracy. Arggggh.

It was time to re-direct my thoughts. I knew the information that I had posted was simply what I knew. Sure, I wished that the Christy boot never happened, but I had to have faith in the rest of my intel. I wasn't exactly sure how it could pan out now, but at this point the game had taken so many turns that anything was possible. Something would happen to pull Butch through to the Final 4. And Matt and Jenna were still going to the F2.

As I lay in bed, I reflected on my time in the Amazon. Was it possible that I had missed something? Was there some clue that might explain why Christy was not going to the Final 4, some sign that might point to what was going to happen next? Mentally, I re-traced my steps through my ENTIRE time at the Ariau and replayed ALL the conversations I had with Enrique and Uncle Boat Driver. Searching, wondering. I rewinded, fast-forwarded, and paused. But I kept coming to the same answer...the same F4. After all, it was written down on a piece of paper for me. It was as clear as black and white.

Still, I kept searching for something odd, something strange...something that just did not seem, well, right. I racked my brain...looking for any indication that this all really might have been a complicated hoax thrust into my eager hands. Could Enrique and Uncle Boat Driver really have been "playing" me? Was it possible that CBS had indeed coached them on just how to handle this type of situation? I didn't even want to think about that, but I knew that when a good covert operator has something go wrong he must ask all the tough questions. But I came up empty. There was nothing there to see. My conversations with my sources had been candid, honest, and sincere. It was misguided to question these two Brazilians' integrity and I wouldn't do it anymore.

So what would I post on my thread Friday morning? The answer was simple, as clear as the F4 names on my piece of paper. I would do what I had been doing all along: tell THE TRUTH. Of course, that was assuming I could still post at all and that Q, the Administrator at the time, had not locked my thread overnight. Ah, but even if that happened I would just start a new thread to finish the season.

I glanced over at my clock...it was almost midnight. I chuckled, rolled over, and fell asleep. And though inside my computer the flames were still crackling, I slept just fine.

On Friday, May 2nd, I woke up a new man. I was ready to do battle, not in an aggressive, flame-war way but in a covert operator's manner of doing battle. I would defend my intel against the overnight flaming, without getting too involved in the BS. It was time to move forward with my spoiler and the game. As much as the previous night was a shock to us all, it was over and done with. I still believed wholeheartedly in my spoiler. I would stand by my F2, and I even would stand by Butch making it to the F4, as improbable as that seemed by the game dynamics. I was ready to post!

First off, I was glad to see my thread was not locked. My strategy was simple. I would filter out the insults and attacks but answer the more intellectual questions. As I opened up my two sessions and began my usual process of cutting and pasting their questions to address in my response post, I was amazed to see just how many inquiries had been directed at me! In fact, so many questions had come in overnight that I had to break up my answers into two posts. I did not want to miss someone because I felt that everyone who posted a reasonable question to me deserved an answer. And I would refrain from any Internet YELL-ING, as much as I might be tempted to lash back. If I stooped to their level, I would gain nothing.

I was so busy crafting my response that I missed the last post to come in before mine that morning. Trixiego was the poster and the tone was all positive:

"ChillOne, I'll reiterate some other posters. You stood by your information, admitted graciously when off and stayed cool with the flaming. I don't doubt your sincerity in the least.

I still think you gave us good information for us to spoil during the course of the season. I personally would never have thought the first two boots would be men.

I personally would never have figured Jenna to get this far.

I personally would not have figured Matt to get this far considering his 'editing' until only recently.

You gave us good info regarding the nudity as well as other 'tidbits.'

...I almost felt with CO 'spoiling' the show it was a 'dead' season. Last night was one of the greatest shows because the information was inaccurate.

Be that as it may, CO kept coming back here and was polite and answered everyone's questions...he assisted in us knowing A LOT more than some of us would have guessed so give him a break. He took a lot of flak and I don't doubt for a minute that he reported the information as he saw it and it wasn't some ridiculous hoax people think it is. After all the seasons with the supposed 'spoilers' I think we can tell the difference between the two.

When this is retired, it deserves a proverbial gold watch."

So that's the last posting anyone would see before I came back "on the air." My post clocked in at 6:28 a.m.:

"Good Morning...

Wow, lots of overnight activity, but expected. Anyway, let me address some of the comments:

MediaDeeva:

Quote: **How can you stand by your spoiler when the whole time it was Butch, Christy, Jenna and Matt final 4? That's gone baby. It's over.**

Simple, I continue to trust my source. And, I will stand by my intel until it is 100% gone. How do you know that Matt, Jenna, and Butch will not make it to the Final 4??? This game is completely dynamic. Alliances can change, immunities can be won, etc. You never know…Unless, of course, you can provide some inside intelligence that these 3 do not make it to the F4…and I'm not talking about speculating about it and not being able to see it. I'm talking hard proof.

and…

Quote: **this was never a good spoiler**

Why??? Just because boot orders were off, doesn't make this a bad spoiler. Back in early January, I provided location information, cast information, game dynamic information. I provided some information about the first group of people to be voted off. My source gave me boot order, so I posted it. That was my intel. Those in my group, although out of order, went out first…did they not??? My source provided a group of people that would last to the end…a Final 4 of people. Did these people all not make it to the end??? Sure, Christy was voted off in 6th place vs. 4th. Why does that make this a bad spoiler??? Don't I still have 3 potential F4 contestants left??? Media-Deeva, please tell me what you think is a 'good spoiler.' I'd like to know. I'm sure others would like to know.

Survivorstillsucks2:

Quote: **ChillOne….you will get real cold standing alone**

No worries, I've got lots of friends out here (believers and non-believers).

Griffe and Sam Buru: Thanks. This is the attitude that many people lack out here.

Jedijake:

Quote: **you are evil-because you aren't who you say you are-PERIOD, END OF DISCUSSION! There's no way around this one, dude (or dudes).**

Negative…discussion is not over. You can't make a bold statement like that without proving it. Don't be a coward and post something, then run away. You have just publicly accused me of being someone I'm not, now, go prove it. Come back when you've got something.

Anti:

Quote: **ChillOne is wrong. He was wrong from day 1. His boot order has been wrong from the start and will almost certainly be wrong the rest of the way now.**

Anti…not all my information was wrong. Boot orders were off, but if you step back and look at the big picture, there were many correct things. This spoiler was not all about boot order. There was a plethora of information that I provided about the show. Please don't let the negative's spoil the positives.

and...

Quote: **I'm so glad it's over**

It's not over until the fat lady sings.' Look, I still have 60% of my F4 still alive. You never know what's going to happen. This spoiler will not be over until Butch, Jenna, and Matt are all voted off and/or win.

and finally...

Quote: **Thanks to Uncle ChillOne for your contributions to our legacy**

Thanks Anti. I promised to keep myself here from head-to-toe and I will continue to keep that promise. You are a gentleman and a scholar.

Wezzie: THANKS!!! You see survivorsucks2, I'm not out here alone.

BBMaxHostFrank:

Quote: **Okay, angry people out there! I think it's time to give ChillOne a BREAK! The man was wrong WOOOOOW!!!**

Appreciate you having my back...this is DEFINITELY a tough crowd.

Back to JediJake:

Quote: **Just a VERY well designed fake spoiler that was planned well before it was planted**

Thank you.

Verizon Calling:

Quote: **His final four is blown out of the water**

Without speculating, prove it...

and

Quote: **Staying at a hotel where none of the employees spoke English**

Have you been to the Ariau???

OK...I'll continue in my next post

—The ChillOne"

That was a start. I showed them I was back and feeling cool, calm, and collected. I was standing up to the fire without backing down. I was challenging them to be factual, to "play" this game for real. I was back in the zone and feeling good. It was 7:08 a.m. when I got back on for my continued responses.

To one poster's comment that a spoiler doesn't have to be 100% correct to be great but just has to "enliven the senses" I said, "My sentiments exactly. There are a lot of 'I told you so's' coming out of the woodwork."

To a question raised about whether people would still call me a hoax if my F2 came true, I replied, "I'd like to know what people think about this as well."

To SamCahill's saying "fuck you" to me, I noted, "Again, tough crowd. Damn. Is this type of post appropriate under the ezboard Terms and Conditions???"

And to a suggestion that the Administrator lock up my thread, I reasoned that such a move would "not make sense. My intel is still very much alive. Again, it ain't over till its over!!! This thread has been the focus of a lot of great *Survivor* conversation this season. And, IMHO, not a waste of space."

There. I could almost feel the fire hoses spraying jets of water across the thread. Most of the big flames were being snuffed out. Yes, the heat was still a bit intense and the ashes would still smolder awhile, and there was certainly some damage under the rubble. But as everyone could see, I was already out there with my tools rebuilding my thread piece by piece. I was moving on, heading for the Final 4.

11

THE FINAL 4

Strategy. Now, more than ever, it was all about strategy. More and more, I found myself comparing my moves on SurvivorSucks to the great gamesmanship of Rob, who was emerging as the smartest contestant on S6. Like Rob, I was determined to think two or three steps ahead. Anticipate danger. Claw my way out of it when it came. Defend myself when necessary while not getting caught up in the emotional side of the game. Understand that I may be liked one minute and disliked the next, even by the same people. Know where I stood at all times, know what my competitors were thinking, and use that knowledge to my advantage. Anticipate the head games and the backstabbing. See the big picture. Look ahead, not behind.

Only a few days after my strategic rebuttals to the flames over the Christy boot shocker, the sentiments of the board had clearly swung my way again. Not only did my thread not get locked, but one of my nastiest critics got booted off the forum. The night after Ep.11, the Administrator told mediadeeva not to post again after a brutal and personal flaming war with Newbie that had tied up the board for hours. Newbie also was directed to take a hike. I just smiled and said nothing. I almost expected it, especially after I had mentioned in my own post earlier that day that "MD's mouth is like that of a drunken sailor." Now the sailor had been sent off to drift out to sea.

I was even more encouraged to see so many other people stepping forward to defend me. Many of these posters explained to the board how my overall intel had helped them succeed in their office and fantasy pools. That was a clear indicator that my information was much more on the mark than off. Many of the lurkers expressed disbelief that my intel was being branded as complete BS when they were poised to rake in big money in their pools by paying close attention to what I had predicted. Of course, I might have been winning some money myself but I did not wager on S6 at all. I had given up sports betting a long time ago and extended the same policy to similar kinds of wagering.

Anyway, although I was no longer feeling at all down in the dumps and had been ready to rock from the first post-Christy morning, it was nice to see more solid signs of support. Even Intelly, my former antagonist, admitted that he "was accused of cheating (inside information) in one of my pools. It seems I used too much of Chilled ones info in frame work of my initial picks." Then Intelly added this interesting food for thought:

"It also has been fun to watch Chilled One and Milkshaky twist and backpedal. Will they become the real survivors?"

Yes, I was striving to become the main survivor in this game-within-the-game on SurvivorSucks, and to this point I had been successful. For four solid months, my spoiler had stood up to every kind of imaginable debate in an environment were my every word was picked apart and analyzed by thousands. I was still alive, steadfast and determined to come out as the Sole Survivor on this thread. If my Final 4 and Final 2 held up, I really would win this game. Only one more episode to go before the finale.

Of course, I had to weather a few more storms even before we got to Ep.12. On one front, the media picked up on the hit I had taken with Christy's boot. Michael Hewitt of *The Orange County Register* followed up on his earlier article that talked up my spoiler by noting that now "it's back to square one, or maybe square two, for the spoilers." And a headline over an update on *Reality News Online* proclaimed: "Vote Against Christy Spoils the Spoilers." The media spin did sting a little, but I understood their game, too. It just served as a reminder that once you become notorious outside your own domain, the attention can be both positive and negative. I could handle it.

I also made a mistake of sorts in trying to spin my way out of the Christy boot error and hedge my bets about the Final 4. Picking up on other posters' speculation that Uncle Boat Driver might have interpreted the Final 4 to actually be the last four contestants voted off before the Final 2 were determined, I speculated that Butch, Matt and Jenna could be the next three boots. That would mean my source was actually correct in his order of the last four "to go," and Rob and Heidi would be left as the actual F2.

OK, maybe I had lost just a bit of confidence in my source at that point, just two days after Christy's exit. In reality, I knew nothing about Uncle Boat Driver's ability to remember details or interpret my questions exactly right. My confidence in him and his intel was based purely on his reaction time and body language when answering my questions. I knew he wasn't making things up. He may have simply remembered wrong when he named Christy as the first survivor in the Final 4, but he also might have been thinking about the show's dynamics in a different way. So I toyed with this speculation briefly, hoping to cover my tracks in the spoiling game. But from the board's skeptical response, I could see that this strategy would not help me. I could not afford to be seen as changing gears this far down the road. So by the morning of May 4th, I steered back to my real intel with this post:

"I find it hard to believe that my source and I were talking about 2 different sequence of boots…me thinking F4, F3, F2, F2 and he thinking F6-F3; although it cannot be ruled out….I will 'stay on intel' and hold to the facts as originally interpreted; w/o miscommunication. I will say that my source just missed the Christy boot and look for Butch (3rd), Matt and Jenna (F2's)."

As the countdown to Ep.12 continued, I was not alone on the board among spoilers trying on different theories to address just how Uncle Boat Driver had gone wrong, or at least how he had missed this one key boot. One reason my source was getting more attention was because one of the Ariau boat drivers could be clearly spotted on TV during Ep.11, and it was apparent that he was close enough to the action of the show to know what was going on. It wasn't actually my Uncle Boat Driver that we all noticed. This boat driver was chubby and my dude was thin as a rail, but the spoilers could see for themselves that I had been right all along in explaining that these Brazilian ferry boat drivers really could have been informed sources.

This kind of exploration into Uncle Boat Driver also was good for my cause, because the focus was no longer just on trying to analyze ME. On May 5th, black light poster presented a highly detailed and very creative "story" about Uncle Boat Driver and the history of my thread. Though I disagreed with many of the points raised, I found the whole thing totally entertaining. Here's part of how it started:

"One night in January 2003 this (C1) and this guy (UBM) had a couple of beers together in the bar inside this semi-cheesy tourist joint (Ariau).

While they're both nice guys, they're from vastly different circumstances in life. This guy (C1), is a young, gung-ho, highly-educated, well-paid, unmarried, Boston-area information systems consultant who globe-hops for both work and pleasure. He can well afford to buy interesting people drinks, and does. He takes pride in being not easy to fool.

This guy (UBM) is a low-paid, poorly-educated, South American boatman who shuttles tourists on the river locally for the resort. There's a good chance he hasn't exactly done a lot of international travel, like the American with the great job and plenty of money has. Possibly he has a wife, and maybe (pic of Brazilian kiddies) another responsibility or two at home to support.

His life may not be very cosmopolitan or even eventful, especially compared to those of rich American tourists'. But he enjoys himself. Enjoys socializing…just shooting the shit, about any unusual thing that may have happened in his life, like anybody does.

He likes talking about (Jenna) 'cute chicks,' especially ones he's seen (naked (Jenna)) And he likes (beer)."

At one point in the story, BLP speculated that Uncle Boat Driver deliberately handed me a false answer here and there because he really was under contract not to share the secrets of *Survivor* and was trying to cover his butt. Wrong. If that was the case, I couldn't imagine my source even sitting at that table with Enrique and me chatting openly about the details of *Survivor: The Amazon* at all.

BLP also wondered if Uncle Boat Driver gave me some answers to some questions, even when he couldn't remember, just to make me a happy Ariau tourist. I had to admit that this could conceivably have been true, but not in BLP's context. My source certainly was trying to answer all or most of my questions, but I didn't think for a minute that he was trying to manipulate his answers. It was far more likely that he was answering my questions and filling in the Final 4 order to the best of his ability, knowing that he was not 100% sure about it but not clarifying that he could be remembering wrong.

BLP continued to chronicle his version of my night with Enrique and Uncle Boat Driver and what happened next on my thread. I did not post any response, but I was reacting as I read at home to points like these:

"The entire evening went well; everyone seemed happy.

Within a few days, though, that conversation's every statement, word, nuance, implication, and significance, or lack thereof, would begin to be inspected and discussed relentlessly by an untold number of people all around the globe…(and) *occupy many people's thoughts for, in total, many thousands of hours."*

That was certainly true. The four months of almost constant postings and activity on my thread spoke volumes about how "hot" my story had become. And it still wasn't over.

"It would cause meetings to be held within a large corporation."

As I mentioned earlier, I could not confirm anything that did or did not happen at CBS and SEG, but I certainly believed this was true. It had to be true. ChillOne had just posted a massive amount of information about S6, a full month before the season premiere. Did CBS accelerate the *TV Guide* spot about *Survivor: The Amazon*? I thought so. Did CBS accelerate the official cast announcement on *The Early Show*? I thought so. Did CBS have to re-strategize its editing patterns for the show in response to my spoiler? I thought so. Was

CBS pissed off about my spoiler? I thought so. Did CBS investigate how it happened? I thought so.

Was CBS, generally speaking, challenged by the ChillOne spoiler? All signs pointed that way. In fact, I believed they welcomed the challenge. It kept them on their toes, and it kept talk about the show fresh. By S6, *Survivor* was facing TONS of competition in reality TV. They had to ensure that *Survivor* kept pace with the likes of *American Idol* and *Joe Millionaire*. I strongly suspected that many people at CBS were getting lots of praise for their efforts in combating my spoiler with editing patterns, possible postings on SurvivorSucks, etc.

BLP also said of my saga on Sucks:

"It would spawn many strongly held, expressed, and debated points of view. It would fire strong emotions, words, and exchanges between people some of whom are continents apart. It would provide the raw material from which some people would come to attack, mock, ridicule, deride, curse, and dislike each other. It would lure crazy people out of lurkdom."

Sure did. IMHO, that's what already made this the best damn thread/spoiler in the history of *Survivor* spoiling! BLP also made me nod in agreement when he made this observation about Internet message boards:

"Such is the strange, new world that became possible in the past ten years when the internet became widely available to the obsessive-compulsive and/or attention-deprived all around the world."

To me, the Internet is the greatest information medium the world has ever seen. Yes, it brings out some strange people. But it also brings thousands of sincere people together into fascinating debates. And despite what some critics may argue about how trivial the many discussion groups on the Internet can be, boards like SurvivorSucks demonstrate just how relevant and important what happens on Internet forums really are at times. As we headed for Ep.12, I just wished more people in the greater fandom of *Survivor* knew what was going on with my thread and were tuning into my spoiler.

Ep.12, "The Amazon Heats Up," May 8: Well, anyone who was aware of the ChillOne spoiler could see that Ep.12 went my way. Jenna was ailing and actually asking to be voted off, but that didn't worry me. The guys were looking at Heidi as the stronger Final 4 threat. So Matt, Rob, and Butch voted to dump Heidi, and she was gone. That left 3 of my F4 still standing. My posting that evening was brief. I simply quoted my earlier post in which I had said:

"If Heidi gets the boot this Thursday, I would admit to my source totally screwing up 4th place and still feel very confident in Butch (3rd) and Jenna and Matt in the F2. I would expect Rob to place 4th, obviously."

To that quote, I simply added, "That is all," and then I left it to the board to handle the post-show analysis. At that point, I knew there wasn't much left to debate. We were just three days and counting until the final episode. With the Final 4 of Butch, Rob, Matt, and Jenna, I felt more strongly than ever that Matt and Jenna would battle it out for the Sole Survivor title. That would mean my intel was the most accurate on the F2, the most celebrated topic. My status on Monster Island would be secured. I could say I really did it!

The three days passed quickly, without too much flak on Sucks. I again witnessed many lurkers coming forward to praise me for helping them win money in office pools. A typical posting on this subject, this one on the morning of May 9th, was the very first by bananaonmydesk:

"After following C1 and a myriad of other spoilers all season without putting in my 2 cents, here it is. C1 has more correct information than anyone else I have seen (and if my employees knew how much time I spent looking I be jobless)…

"…I am winning the office pool thanks to him. And I'd venture to say that many others are also….

"If you listened to what C1 said, and tried to interpret it you should be able to get 8/10 boots correct. If you overthink it and start trying to second guess, you screwed up. At least that worked for me."

I actually did not realize there were so many *Survivor* office pools out there. I guess making pools for *Survivor* has become almost as big as the pools for March Madness—the college basketball championship. It was nice to know I was helping some people who followed my spoiler, and I loved hearing them thank me. When it comes to receiving thanks and praise, the more the merrier. But as I read more of these pats on the back before the S6 finale, I wondered about a couple of things. First, was I now hearing from the "silent majority" of readers of my thread? Could it really have been true that, even with all the flames from all my critics, most people following ChillOne really did believe in it but were perhaps intimidated by the vociferous non-believers? I had to think that was possible.

But I also had to wonder whether some of these compliments might have been coming from someone using an alias to cover their real Sucks identity. Maybe some of these "browsers" were really some of my former critics finally wanting to publicly acknowledge me for being mostly right, without having to eat crow under their main alias. Just imagining the possibility made me laugh.

For all of us in this large and lively virtual community, we knew our time was soon coming to an end. Like the contestants on *Survivor: The Amazon*, we were already reflecting back on the whole experience. A couple of observations from infrequent posters caught my eye. The first was from RiverD:

"...if it weren't for this spoiler, no matter how it turns out, we'd have all been reading thread after thread, analyzing CBS clues until our brains friend, and arguing over anything and everything else under the sun. If nothing else, this has been a fine campground."

Yep, I had to agree. *Survivor* is a fun show to watch, but it's really not supposed to behave like a spoiler generator. The show is edited to keep the general public's curiosity alive...to make people want to come back week after week, episode after episode, to watch and see what's going to happen. That's the lure of reality TV: curiosity. That's also the driving force behind the genesis of spoiling: over-curiosity, addiction.

If all the spoilers ever had were the clues given to them by CBS, they would have nothing more than bits and pieces and not get very far. And yes, CBS does sometimes slip and give away secrets that were not intended. To some spoilers, that type of information is enough. But for the greater majority, that's not nearly enough. Enter spoilers like ChillOne. Spoilers who deliver information above and beyond what was meant to be known, while giving the *Survivor* spoiling fan base MUCH more to work with or even spoon-feeding some. I felt fully satisfied in knowing that I had brought home from my Amazon vacation the most solid and extensive base of material that had ever come down this pike.

Had it been worth it for me? That's what Karma wanted to know in a supporting post:

"I haven't posted that much on this thread, but I've read every page. (Which is more, I'm sure, than can be said for many of the shriekers). It's been quite a ride.

So Thanks, ChillOne, for your dedication and perseverance thru all the crap. I sincerely hope that, in the end, you feel it was worth the time and effort you put into it; and that you had some fun."

You better believe it was worth it! And the ride was not over. The three-hour season finale of *Survivor: The Amazon* was set for the evening of Sunday, May 11th. The real fun was still to come.

12

UNCLE BOAT DRIVER'S REDEMPTION

To the spoiling community, I was ChillOne, a guy who for four months had calmly answered all relevant questions put to him, patiently dismissed the same rumors about being a plant or a hoax over and over again, and resiliently stood his ground against wave after wave of flaming. But in my Boston apartment on the night of the final episode of *Survivor: The Amazon*, I could just be me. A guy hanging out with his brother and one of his oldest friends, with a fridge stocked with ice-cold beer. It was time to get this party started!

Everything was in its place in my living room. My 36-inch, flat-screen TV, hooked-up to my Dolby 5.1 surround sound system, was cranked and ready. A few Indian artifacts that I purchased in the Amazon were propped around the room, providing an appropriate jungle theme. On my walls were some of my favorite scenes: A big Andreas Feininger print of Route 66 in Arizona, maybe my favorite place and a state I may settle down in someday. A painting of the fourth hole at Bethpage Black, home of the 2002 U.S. Open, a course that I play every year. Three Christy Edwards watercolors of the ferryboats that I captain from Long Island to Fire Island in the part-time summer job that I've held for the past 18 years.

Yes, my friend Puddin' Head, my brother, and I were totally psyched for the grand finale. In my own home base, with people who knew me as a different name than ChillOne, I was free to cheer for Matt and Jenna as loud as I wanted. I could jump up and down as I pleased. I could scream, "NO!" if anything went wrong with my intel, or exchange hive-fives with Puddin' Head if it all went well. I could even mutter a few fitting comments to my SurvivorSucks critics, if I chose to. I was totally pumped for the night to begin.

And what a night it was! I was fully confident right from the start. Even when Butch, Matt, and Rob made a guy's pact to oust Jenna, I didn't worry at all. I figured she would win the necessary Immunity Challenge to stay alive. I didn't even mind much when Butch, not Rob, was voted off in fourth place, even though my intel had Butch tabbed for third. After all, all eyes were on the Final 2. And when Rob, Matt, and Jenna took that seaplane ride above the Amazon jungle area, I was thrilled to see such a panoramic shot of the same jungle locales that I had visited. For the three remaining survivors, it was the land where they had lived in trying to win the game. For me, it was the land I had roamed with my sources, discreetly trying to spoil what happened in the real game of *Survivor*. It made for great memories for all of us, and I soaked in mine.

When Jenna won the final Immunity, I knew I was home free. She voted Rob off, and my F2 was there! Jenna and Matt. Matt and Jenna. My source had been right all along. Uncle Boat Driver, despite errors in memory that left my other boot picks tantalizing close but not quite right, had nailed the biggest prize of all! And by posting it all a month before the show, I had become the conduit of the biggest and earliest spoiler to pan out in its final act.

On to the *Survivor: The Amazon* reunion in New York City for the final vote to determine the Sole Survivor. A few weeks earlier, some posters on my thread had urged me to go to New York to see it live and in person, but I was totally content to be just where I was. And feeling good about the outcome. Jenna, the F2 contestant that my source had said was better liked, was going to prevail. The Final 4 member that I had listed as first in order of longevity would win the final Tribal Council vote. No, I never directly said Jenna would win that dramatic final vote against Matt. But I sure did HINT at it.

When Jeff Probst held up the card with the fourth vote for Jenna, clinching her victory, I let out one big cheer that, had I been back at the Ariau, would have had the monkeys screeching. Maybe even a louder cheer than the night in April when I watched Syracuse, my alma mater, won the college basketball National Championship. And after a few triumphant moments in the privacy of my own Boston home, it was time to tune into my second "home" on SurvivorSucks. Isgal1 had the first post:

"*ChillOne You Rule*
Clap clap clap clap"

A few minutes later, erickman added:

"*boatman was right they liked Jenna better*"

While some die-hard flamers still wouldn't admit defeat, that just stirred others to go after them. As PabloMax put it:

"*Sheesh, you people are tough. This guy got the final two, and hinted at the winner, weeks before the show even hit the air! And some of you are still ragging on him.*"

I give the guy credit for producing one of the best spoilers ever."

And then, at 10:38 p.m. on that wonderful Sunday night, Intelly showed up and saluted me:

"My XXXXXXXXXX

XX

XX

XX

XX

XXXXXXXXXXXXXXXXXXX'S

OFF TO YOU! GOOD JOB

INTELLY"

Ah, Intelly. We had been back and forth over the course of time, with a few snarls as head-to-head opponents at first, to a bit more respect, and then finally to acceptance and even appreciation. Had Intelly been in my room, I could see us shaking hands like Daniel and Roger during the S6 reunion show after their earlier bickering in the Amazon. Like the 16 contestants on S6, we all had been through a lot together on SurvivorSucks.

The tributes continued to pour in. From jaxwax:

"Out of all the spoilers I have seen on these boards year after year, your spoiler was the BEST!

It was the most complete. It was the most accurate. It was by far the most informative.

Granted I used it with a little intuition, but I used it in my pool and finished #1. I have you to thank for that.

Hope to see you again in S7! Great job and thanks again."

Then from survr iii africa:

"Although there have been several who have bashed you along the way, this season wouldn't have been the same without you and your spoilers. It turned out that you were correct about your final two and nobody else would have chosen those two Survivors to be in the end. Even though some things didn't happen the way that you said, it wasn't your fault and you outspoiled anyone in the history of this board."

At 11:10, it was Uncle Edna's turn:

"I agree…this deserves a nice, comfortable spot in Monster Island. Well done, even though I'm in the ranks of the naysayers."

Still before midnight, rogerdon41 chimed in:

"Great job C1!!! You were right about just enough to make reading your posts and watching Survivor all the more fascinating. And Jenna won, and I am very happy for her."

Of course, Jenna was not the most well liked person by everyone in the TV audience or the spoiler rooms. I did like and respect her, but I'll be honest. I was rooting for her and Matt to reach the F2 and for Jenna to win basically because of my intel. Had I been a more casual fan, I would have been rooting for my home-town boy Rob. I spent 34 years of my life on Long Island and still consider myself a Long Islander. My parents still live there. All of my closest friends are there. That's where I spend most of my spare time. I just happen to live in Boston for now. Also, Rob played the game so well.

As the season went on, I could understand why some people didn't like Jenna. As she admitted to Jeff Probst during the reunion show, she could come across as spoiled or annoying, but she was "learning." A few posters who did admit to dis-liking Jenna personally said that her victory was acceptable because of ME. As my trusted and consistent supporter Orangeena put it, "the only thing that made it bearable was it proved your F2 right."

That one touched me. I liked knowing others out there were rooting for me. In our game-with-the-game, they wanted me to prevail and my critics to fall. A poster named pirahnna 8 my scrotum (again, I could never be sure if this was a second alias for someone better known) added:

"Chill, if I wore a hat, it would be off to you. You handed these guys the best spoiler ever, and some dorks tried to crucify you for it. The laugh's on them. Great job."

Were my former critics in great pain over the end result? Did I want them to be suffering? Nah, not really. In the end, I was the one who had the last laugh. That's the only thing that mattered to me. The flamers had lost the battle. After all the spoiling, all the flame wars, all the debates, all the speculation, and the 4,000-plus posts, I had made it to the end. I didn't even post myself that night. After my final episode party with Puddin' Head and my bro had wound down, I just said to myself, "Jenna won, and so did ChillOne." I smiled and got ready for bed. What I most wished is that no matter what my critics still might say pub-licly, they understood the true magnitude of what had just happened. As Oshun Anat noted:

"No one has ever done as much damage spoiling wise in all six seasons of Survivor, and I wonder if we'll ever see this kind of spoiler again."

Well, that was my hope from Day One. I wanted to the biggest ever. Even on that January flight back to the U.S. from Brazil, I had said to myself, "I'm gonna knock their socks off with this! Whoever reads my intel—whether they be spoil-ers, the media, spies from CBS, or whoever—will remember this spoiler for a long, long time."

Back then, not having lived in the spoiling world, I did not know much of the historical competition I would be judged against. I had heard of Gervase X but did not know anything about most of the others. As I got more involved in SurvivorSucks, I became better educated on a few of the other more memorable spoilers.

Going back to S1, Gervase X was not the only hot spoiler story. Another one that energized the spoiling community was "Black Gretchen." This one originated from a vidcap of the opening montage of one of the seasons early episodes, back when Executive Producer Mark Burnett probably didn't think anyone would pay such close attention to everything he showed. During that episode, he edited in a split-second shot of nine people seated at Tribal Council. By analyzing the contestants in that clip, spoilers deduced that the scene was from an episode *after* the two tribes had merged. This allowed spoilers to work backwards to identify the first seven survivors to be voted off.

But the busy spoilers ran into one tough obstacle. They could not definitively identify one of those nine survivors. Was that murky figure Gervase, an African-American male? Or was it really Gretchen, a white female? Strange as it seemed, those were the two most logical options. While spoilers zoomed-in for close-ups and analazyed them for clues, they dubbed this mysterious figure "Black Gretchen." For awhile, it was the hottest topic on the boards. But the mystery was cleared up on Ep.7 when Gretchen was voted off, revealing Gervase to be the previously unidentified contestant.

S2 (Australia) saw the emergence of an online group called the Ellipsiiis Brain Trust. They gained a reputation by picking almost every boot and challenge winner correctly during the second half of the season. That stirred a debate in the spoiling world, of course. Were they just damn good spoilers? Or could they have had a source inside the show? The rumors flared, and the media picked up on the group's success. Like me, the Ellipsiiis Brain Trust also faced a bunch of attackers, many of whom complained about the group's holier-than-thou attitude. But in S3, the Ellipsiiis Brain Trust lost its touch. After error upon error, they broke up. The other S2 spoiler was the famous Uncle Camerman, whom I already mentioned.

Sometimes the spoiling community would get wrapped up in strange clues that CBS was sprinkling in. One example focused on the "Neleh reversals" in S4 (Marquesas). A poster named NelehWillWin explained that Neleh was named after her grandmother Helen—that is, "Neleh" spelled backwards. During the S4 season, MB edited certain footage to include strangely out-of-sequence shots and momentary backward images. For example, one vidcap showed Neleh's face; her scar was on her right cheek and her mole on her left. But in a second vidcap, MB's edits had them switched while the "CBS watermark" had remained in place. That clearly was not the work of any online prankster. But would it hold up all the way to a Neleh victory in the Final 2?

Well, many spoilers thought so because they believed that MB did that kind of thing all of the time. Turn the clock back to S3 (Africa). In that season, a spoiler by the name of Tapewatcher developed an intriguing story based on what he saw as Biblical allusions surrounding the long-haired, bearded, and Jewish contestant Ethan. Ethan would frequently be edited to include an image resembling the Star of David. Right from the first episode, Ethan was depicted with crosses and stars all over the place. He even stumbled during a challenge, just as Jesus stumbled carrying the cross. "Follow the Star", and you will find the winner, Tapewatcher predicted. He was oddly correct. Ethan did win the $1 million prize for that *Survivor* season.

So it made sense, to many, that the Neleh reversals similarly pointed to Neleh winning it all in S4. But it turned out that MB had been highlighting Neleh to throw the spoilers off. Neleh wound up placing second to the Sole Survivor, Vecepia. MB never showed any clues pointing to a Vee triumph at any point of the season. After she won, he started talking about her great game strategy, while fans were feeling cheated!

To bring spoiling history all the way up to the last previous show before *Survivor: The Amazon*, the main spoiler during S5 (Thailand) was TrueDorkTimes breaking the news of a Brian/Clay F2 with a few weeks still left in that season. With S6 coming on the heels of that successful spoiler, many theorists interpreted Jenna's negative editing as an attempt by MB to throw people off the ChillOne spoiler. If he convinced enough people that Jenna couldn't win, maybe they wouldn't believe I had it nailed all along.

There have been other spoilers here and there, and there surely will be more.

But I had to agree with Oshun Anat. The ChillOne spoiler had made a name for himself and had proved worthy of legendary spoiler status. Personally, I do not think a legendary spoiler should be based purely on accuracy of F4 picks anyway. There are many other components that should be analyzed. Sure, the F4 and F2 are important, and so is overall accuracy, but let's look at some other factors:

- When did the spoiler come out? To me, the earlier the better. Someone who comes out two days before an episode and says that person X is going to be voted off does not hold much water, except maybe for Snewser who is well respected because he does it all the time. However, if spoiler Y comes along and predicts a boot months in advance, that's much more of a story.

- How much information was revealed? To me, a spoiler that has a great deal of information is much more memorable than a spoiler that only has a few tidbits.

- How accurate did it prove to be? A spoiler can certainly be a hoax. And memorable spoilers can certainly be hoaxes, but the truly legendary spoilers must also include a solid dose of accuracy, too.

- How much media attention did it get? Simply, did the spoiler grow beyond its thread status and hit other media entities? Did it have a life outside the bounds of its own forum?

- Did it make it to Monster Island, a.k.a., The Spoiling Hall of Fame, or the equivalent in some other spoiling forum?

Based on all these criteria, did ChillOne become #1? I thought so, but I may have been just a little biased. But based on many a comment on my thread, I wasn't alone in my conclusion. Again, what made my spoiler so different from ALL the others was the fact that it included SO MUCH information and was presented SO FAR in advance, over a month before the premiere. Nothing like this had ever happened and most likely never will happen again. Only a true CBS insider could do as much damage as ChillOne at this point, and time is running out. *Survivor* won't be around forever. Who knows? Maybe the all-star *Survivor 8* will be the last. The window of opportunity that opened up for me now has been closed. CBS, no doubt, has made sure of that.

So with my work complete and my status assured, there wasn't much left for me to say to the board. My post on Monday morning, May 12th, at 7:01 a.m., was my sign-off:

"CONGRATULATIONS to Jenna for being the Sole Survivor!!!

GOOD JOB to Butch, Rob, and Matt for getting as far as you did.

Thanks to all of the other S6 contestants for making this installment the best season to date.

FINALLY KUDOS to everyone who has come to this thread. I've enjoyed my time out here and glad to have "met" all of you. I wish all of you luck in your future endeavors.

On to Survivor 7 and beyond...

—The ChillOne"

Still playing "the game," I was clearly letting my results speak for themselves. I was also striving for a classy ending. I didn't give any extra thanks to my supporters or any extra flames to the flamers because there were no sides anymore. I had survived. Period. And I saluted Jenna and the other F4 contestants because I figured they were reading my post and I wanted to make a good impression. Strategy. Got to think two or three steps ahead.

On the spoiling boards, everyone was already anticipating the next *Survivor* series, S7, to be filmed on the Pearl Islands off the coast of Panama. Orangeena had speculated that after my major success, a bunch of ChillOne wannabes would flock to the site looking for their own Uncle Boat Driver source. Of course, CBS would probably be prepared for them.

What about me? Was ChillOne considering another covert intelligence operation? Had I already scoped out a possible trip to the Pearl Islands? Am I working on unlocking the super-secret location of S8 and planning a future mission there? Well, my real plans would need to remain confidential. But one thing I could say for sure: I would be back on the spoiler boards someday. Spoiling was now in my blood.

13

OMAHA CHILL

I was roaming around with some fellow spoilers in a conference room of Harrah's Council Bluffs casino complex, located along the Missouri River just over the Iowa border from Omaha, Nebraska. My eyes were fixated on the entourage of *Survivor: The Amazon* contestants parading into the room. Daniel was carrying the banner for the S6 group, and accompanying him were fellow contestants Dave, Christy, Alex, Heidi, Rob, and S6 Sole Survivor Jenna. As they approached the stage set up with a rock-like background to look like a Tribal Council site, Rob nudged Jenna with his elbow and pointed to me in the audience.

"That's him," I could almost hear Rob whispering. "That's ChillOne."

When Jenna made eye contact with me, I lifted my Heineken and held it out in her direction. Cheers! The winner of the spoiling season was saluting the winner of *Survivor 6*. Then Jenna tugged on Heidi's shirt and motioned toward me as if to say, "Hey, that's ChillOne over there." When they both looked my way, I raised my beer again to both of them.

The "Festival of Reality Superstars," a charity event to benefit AIDS-related causes, was underway. After welcoming remarks from John Carroll, a former survivor and the event's organizer, contestants representing all six *Survivor* seasons broke up for the meet-and-greet "Go Tribal" segment of the evening. Jenna and Heidi were drawing the biggest crowd from the 200 or so *Survivor* fans there, and it wasn't just because Jenna was the $1 million winner of the most recent *Survivor* series. She and Heidi, fresh from their nude scene in S6, also were currently displayed together on the cover of *Playboy*.

Dressed more like typical 20-something casually hip and fashionable women, rather than provocative-looking *Playboy* models, Jenna and Heidi were welcoming fans by shaking hands, signing autographs, and handing out *Survivor* souvenir items. I waited my turn in line. When I got to the front I said simply, "Hey guys, I'm ChillOne."

"ChillOne, I hate you. You're evil," Jenna said as she pointed a menacing finger at me. "You ruined it."

"Ah, I spoiled it, not ruined it," I laughed. "And you ruined the start of my Final 4 when you gave that immunity necklace to Heidi. She was supposed to get voted off the night Christy was booted."

"Oh, that didn't matter," Heidi insisted. "Jenna just gave that to me for insurance purposes. Christy was gone anyway."

And with that, we all shared a laugh. A spoiler and the subjects of his intel had come together, and there was, more than anything, a sense of mutual respect. I gracefully backed off so the other fans in line could get their turn with their *Survivor* favorites.

Hours earlier, I had taken advantage of an opportunity to sit down with Rob, dubbed by host Jeff Probst as the best player never to have won *Survivor*. I was sitting with fellow spoilers Sam Buru, Wezzie, Bon Scott, and Quartzeye when Wezzie beckoned Rob to join us.

"Rob, meet ChillOne," as Wezzie introduced us.

"So you're ChillOne," Rob said. "I know all about you."

Wezzie had met Rob and some of other S6 survivors the previous evening when some of the fans and contestants were arriving in town early. That afternoon, Sam had told me that Daniel said he wanted to beat me up for picking him to get booted first, Jenna wanted to punch me for spoiling her win, and Rob just wanted to meet me. So now Rob and I chatted.

"So how did you come up with the name of ChillOne?" he asked.

I explained that it was close to my nickname from growing up in Long Island, also his home. I noted that the names you really wanted were usually gone on ezboard, and he nodded. Rob told me it took him six or seven tries to find an available name he could accept, Robfather Part II, when he came onto Survivor-Sucks to interact with fans after the show. Rob had been a big *Survivor* fan before he went on S6, but he was just learning about posting life in the spoiling world.

"I couldn't believe the flaming we got there," he said. "They even called Heidi and Jenna whores and sluts."

"Tell me about it," I said. "They flamed me for four months. You just learn to answer what you want to, blow the rest off, and try to be cool about it all."

As we talked, I found Rob to be extremely open, outgoing, candid, and approachable. So were Jenna and Heidi when I met them that evening. These were good people stepping out from their reality TV roles to mingle with fans. A great bunch of folks to have been spoiling.

I had come to this June 2003 conference because it felt important to make personal contact with those characters I had been making predictions about since my intel-gathering visit to their S6 site in January. It also fit part of my new project. I knew I was going to write this book, and I wanted to gain some new exposure for ChillOne. And fortunately, I found both my fellow spoilers and the *Survivor* contestants eager to meet me. They obviously had been carrying lots of questions: Just who was this ChillOne anyway? What did he look like? How did he act? And just how did he uncover the secrets of *Survivor: The Amazon* anyway?

Judging by the typical reaction, I'd conclude that people were surprised at what they found. Perhaps they were expecting an awkward-looking high school kid, or some over-zealous trekkie-type. Instead, they found that outside his Internet persona, ChillOne was really the 30-something, normal-looking, composed guy he had described himself to be on his SurvivorSucks thread. Yes, I was for real.

"NO WAY!!! You're ChillOne? Get out of here!" was how Dave put it when he met me.

Daniel, like Jenna, had to make a dig. "How could you say I was going off first? All my friends believed you," he said, referring to my intel that had Daniel as first boot. "But I have to admit, it did make me look better when I made it to the third episode."

When any of the S6 contestants asked anything about how I had spoiled the show, I delivered my prepared response. It went something like this:

"I was just in the right place at the right time. I was just going to Rio to party with some buddies for New Year's. I had no intention of spoiling *Survivor* until I got to the Ariau. Then I stumbled upon the set and found a couple of people who had been overlooked by CBS who were more than happy to tell me what had been going on with the production. They took me to the Tribal Council site and I could see where you guys went when you were voted off. I went to the challenge area. I was all over the place."

They seemed surprised that my spoiling was not part of some pre-planned venture, and even more surprised that it was so easy for me to find people who would talk so openly about the show. They knew well from their own experience, and the strict contracts they had to sign, just how secretive the whole *Survivor* production can be.

When my fellow spoilers asked me how I did it, I was even briefer in my response. To a spoiler named STLDeb, I smiled and said simply, "You'll have to read my book to find out."

As the opening night activities continued, I also met Lex, one of the more popular contestants from S3 (Africa). As it turned out, he also knew of my reputation even though he was not one of the S6 contestants because his wife was a big *Survivor* fan and frequent visitor to the spoiling community websites. It was nice to hear that at least one former contestant had been attuned to our spoiling world. Alex from S6 happened to be hanging around Lex when I met him. Like Dave, Alex was pretty shocked to meet me.

"Holy shit dude, I know you!" Alex blurted out. "What…is…up!" We shook hands, toasted our beers, BS'ed a little bit, and went our separate ways.

Later that evening, I decided I would try to win one of the items up for auction. All the survivors had brought back something from their time in the Amazon, or something that represented their experience there. Rob was offering some sort of hand-crafted Brazilian belt. I passed on that. I was more intrigued by something Heidi had stuffed in a plastic bag. It turned out to be the jump rope she had brought with her to the Amazon from home as a symbol of her physical education background. The bidding started at about $20, and when I bid $110 I knew I would win. The jump rope had a nasty stench from wherever it had been stashed in the Amazon for more than a month, but I was glad to have it and pleased to have made the contribution to charity.

Still, I wished I had known what was coming soon afterward. It was an 8-ball, not the one Rob had brought to the Amazon as his personal item but another one that the entire S6 cast had signed. So I didn't get that group memento, but I still had all the memories of what I had done in the spoiling world related to this group of good people.

When the program ended for the night, most of the survivors headed off to spend time among themselves at the casino. I hung out with Wezzie and Quartz-eye for awhile and then called it a night.

The next morning, I arrived back at Harrah's after a taxi ride from my Omaha hotel about 9:30. The first conference program of this second and last day started at 10 in a grassy field behind the hotel and casino. One of the local radio stations was conducting a talent show, with the winner bound for New York and a chance to compete for a record contract. The survivors all were manning individual stations at Autograph Island. In a parking lot across from the field, younger *Survivor* fans were playing *Survivor*-like games. Occasionally, I would run into Jenna. Each time, she gave me her pointed finger and evil look. I would just snicker. It became our running gag for the weekend.

At midday, I found my place at the $100 VIP Luncheon. A small group of fans were seated at individual tables with two contestants from one of the *Survi-*

vor seasons. I didn't mind not winding up with any of the S6 cast because Ethan and T-Bird from S3 (Africa) turned out to be excellent company at our table. Ethan, the $1 million winner from his season, was a former soccer player. When I learned that he was a goalie, I told him, "Ahhh, my opponent. I was a goal scorer. I played left-wing my entire soccer life." I found T-Bird to be fun, easy to talk to, and one of the most beautiful people I had ever met. The rest of our table consisted of *Survivor* spoilers like me.

Since neither Ethan nor T-Bird knew much about spoiling, it was our opportunity to educate survivors on this growing cultural phenomenon. We began by filling Ethan in about "Follow the Star"—the Star of David that seemed to follow him around, the stumbling like Jesus with the cross, and Tapewatcher's prediction of his victory based on these edits.

"Mark Burnett does that sort of thing all the time," Quartzeye explained. "The way he edits the show is a way to tell a story within the story, and his use of symbols is amazing. I think he's an editing genius, a big factor in the huge success of *Survivor*. Also, it's his genius that keeps him on his toes, to balance using these clues to keep the general viewing audience intrigued while using it to combat potential spoilers...like ChillOne's."

Ethan was totally blown away. He said he was aware of the Jesus reference but that as many times as he had watched the tapes from his season, he had never noticed the symbolism. He couldn't wait to get home and check it out for himself. T-Bird seemed even more amazed and asked question after question about the entire spoiling culture and how we deciphered our clues. I took their interest as an opening to approach Ethan about the new Reality Central TV cable channel due to launch in January 2004. I had heard he was one of the investors.

"Why not include a weekly feature on Reality Central News focusing on the top Internet spoiling stories and other message board gossip as an alternative *Survivor* preview for that week's episode?" I asked him. "I think it's time for the spoiling community to be more recognized through TV and not just the Internet. Reality Central would be the perfect medium. You know, there are hundreds of fascinating conversations going on from week-to-week, talk that would offer an intriguing mix to the day's top reality stories. I'd be happy to draft a proposal of my pitch."

Ethan said that he thought it was an interesting idea, but he was not involved in the programming or production decisions. He was just an investor, but he might pass my proposal along. Still, I was encouraged to think of the possibilities. Spoiling was growing. The media, even *The New York Times,* was picking up on it. Perhaps ChillOne had played a part in helping to elevate the stature of spoiling by coming on a month before the show and spoiling so much detailed information about the dynamics and outcome of *Survivor: The Amazon*. If I could help take spoiling to the next level, I would consider it a privilege to continue my mission that way....

The main afternoon event brought the *Survivor* contestants back together for a talent competition that resembled *Survivor* challenges. Teams from each season were paired off against each other, so S6 faced S5 (Thailand). The survivors had to navigate an obstacle course, run over a balance beam, put a bucket of water over their heads and work their way through a zigzag maze of cones, spill the water into the bucket, and then get on stilts and move a team member on a stretcher back to the starting point. One of the more amusing highlights was seeing Daniel get over the balance beam without falling and then pumping his fist to the crowd, a signal that he had gotten past his fall on that first challenge of *Survivor: The Amazon*. S6 actually lost to S5, but no one seemed to care. They had put on a good show.

After it was over, the survivors went off to hang with other survivors, the fans went home, and we spoilers headed out for an Omaha steak dinner. I didn't bump into any S6 cast members until Sunday morning at the airport. I was with Sam Buru when we noticed Heidi walk into the coffee shop just ahead of us. A hat partly covered her eyes but her *Survivor: The Amazon* backpack was clearly visible. Some TSA employees were obviously checking her out and whispering to one another. Heidi chatted with us again.

"That jump rope of yours *really* stinks," I laughed.

"I told you," she said with a grin.

She talked more about her plans. Soon she'd be heading off for nursing school in Texas. For Heidi, Jenna, Rob, and the rest of the cast of *Survivor: The Amazon*, it was time to focus on the future. Reunions like this one were great. They would always be survivors and share that special camaraderie and bond with those who had been through it with them. But there were new endeavors to devote their time and energy to, new challenges and decisions to face. *Survivor*, perhaps, had opened a door, but it was up to them to determine where it led.

And so it was for me. As I sat back on the plane headed to Boston, I thought about what was next for ChillOne. For one thing, I would tell my story through this book. Pursuing a part-time writing opportunity for Reality Central would be an intriguing prospect for sure. Beyond that? Well, my eyes would be open to possibilities. An informant never knows when an invitation or an opportunity will call him to duty. And if the call brought me back into the sphere of *Survivor* again, I would be ready and willing to answer it. If there were a banner to carry at the head of some parade of spoilers someday, I would certainly be honored to be considered as one who might carry it. Spoiling *Survivor* in any fashion would always be a juicy challenge because in one way or another it would bring me into the path of Mark Burnett, a worthy adversary indeed. What was it that I had read that MB had said about spoilers once? Something about how we actually help to preserve the secrets of *Survivor* better because of all our different analyses and conflicting opinions about who would win. He even said he found the whole spoiling world fun.

Keeping the secret better? Well, that's what he said back in December 2002. But would MB have made his comment in mid-January 2003, after ChillOne had showed up and blown the lid off of so much of what would happen in *Survivor: The Amazon*? Hmmmm. MB had one thing right, though. It sure was fun!

ACKNOWLEDGEMENTS

The easiest way to thank all the people who played a important role in making this book a reality might just be to reprint the alias' of everyone who posted in my "ChillOne's Amazon Vacation Spoilers" thread on SurvivorSucks. Since that would generate several pages of names, I'll just simply send out a blanket thank-you. Don't forget to visit me on Monster Island!

Writing a book is like nothing I've ever done before. It was a far greater challenge than I ever imagined. When I first thought about this project, three people immediately come to mind that provided the initial encouragement I needed to embark on this journey. To Puddin' Head, Little Louis, and Katherine: Thanks for the support. Thanks for being great friends.

There are a few spoilers who deserve a special mention. To Antithesys, jamesriver, Lexie, MadBananaRush, MissWendyWings, Murtz, Snewser, TrueDorkTimes, and VolcanicGlass: Thank you all for your input.

Dan Bollinger. Thank you as well.

To the cast of S6, especially those of you I met in Omaha, thanks for making *Survivor: The Amazon* the best season to date.

The Omaha gang: Wezzie, Quartzeye, Sam Buru, Bon Scott, The Very Insane Shark, Darrell, STLDeb, QuantumT1, golf99, and the peeps at Voted Off. It was a pleasure meeting you. Thanks for becoming my newest friends.

John Carroll. I appreciated the opportunity to personally buzz my book at your event. Thank you.

Capt. Petey G, the man to be. Thanks for your advice.

To my boys Shep Dog, The O.D.D., K-Flex, and Taff: Looking forward to our next New Year's adventure. Argentina and Uruguay look out!

Finally, I must thank my family, friends, and editor for reading draft after draft of this manuscript. I want you to know how grateful I am to you.

The ChillOne
Boston, Massachusetts
September, 2003

0-595-29178-3

Made in the USA